To Ruby Carlile
In appreciation for
the many years of service
with Christ United Methodist
Women - You are an inspiration to
all of us. We hope you will enjoy this true
story. Written by Dr. Susan Ruby Lamb.
May God bless you for many
more years.

Lady Nellis, UMW President
2012

Stained Glass Windows above the Chancel and Altar in the Sanctuary of Christ United Methodist Church, Memphis, Tennessee.

Christ Church
A Venture in Faith

History of Christ United Methodist Church
Memphis, Tennessee
1955-1985

by
Susan Ruby Breland Lamb

Published by
Christ United Methodist Church
Memphis, Tennessee

First Edition

First Printing—April, 1986

ISBN: 0-9616507-0-2

Printed by
Wimmer Brothers, Inc.
Memphis, Tennessee

Christ Church
A Venture in Faith

History of Christ United Methodist Church
Memphis, Tennessee
1955-1985
by
Susan Ruby Breland Lamb

Editor
Jane Isbell Haynes
Chair, History and Records Committee
Christ United Methodist Church

About the Author

Susan Ruby Breland Lamb (Mrs. Wayne A. Lamb) is a native of Mississippi, a graduate of Taylor University with a Masters Degree in English from Columbia University and a Doctor of Letters Degree from Lambuth College. By profession she is a teacher, having taught in many areas of the Methodist Church. She has also been a worker and leader in United Methodist Women and was the author of their Centennial History, *The Spreading Flame*. She has been a delegate to both the General and Jurisdictional Conferences and has served on the General Council on Ministries. For the past fifteen years she has been the Secretary of the International Foundation of Ewha Woman's University in Seoul, Korea and presently is President-designate of its Board of Directors.

Contents

List of Illustrations

Acknowledgements

Words seem inadequate to express appreciation for all the information and service that has been given by individuals and groups in the preparation and writing of *The History of Christ United Methodist Church*.

We are deeply indebted to the first Committee on History, composed of Mrs. W. J. Templeton (Elizabeth), Mrs. F. M. Ridolphi (Rinne), and Mrs. P. B. Whitenton (Ethel), who served so admirably, and who prepared the history of the first eleven years by recording the events of the Church organization and development. Their work is a valuable document and is on file in the Archives of the Church. We are also indebted to Mrs. W. C. Smith (Frances) for her work as Historian during recent years in making notes on important events, savings newspaper clippings, bulletins and *Couriers* that contained information of historical significance.

We owe a debt of gratitude to Ben Carpenter for the pictures that are used in the *History*. Through the years he has taken pictures of all the events outstanding in the life of Christ Church and has preserved an excellent pictorial history.

We have relied heavily on a number of resource persons who have granted interviews, prepared written information and answered many telephone calls to supply information to insure accuracy. We are fortunate to have Dr. Charles W. Grant and five members of the Steering Committee still active in the life of the Church. The five members of the original Steering Committee are E. C. Handorf, Lee McCormick, Samuel H. Mays, Fred Ridolphi, and James H. Seabrook, Sr. For information regarding buildings and construction, we conferred with E. R. Richmond, Sr., Chairman of the Sanctuary Building Committee. Another resource person has been Reverend Howard Rash who has been an Associate Minister on the staff for more than twenty years. Other members of the church staff have been of inestimable assistance in providing records, names, pictures and other related information. We are grateful to Gynette Bennett, Jan Conder, Mary Ann Thurmond, Denice Hampton, Emily McAllister, Marvin Budd, Jewel Crowson, Shirley Lynn, Mary Gissendanner Marino, and two retired members of the staff, Avis Allen and Glenn Ragland. To all of these, plus all of the other members of the church staff who have given loving and sympathetic support, we say a heartfelt thank you.

There are no words adequate to express our thanks to Laurie Beckwith for the long hours spent in professionally putting the manuscript through several evolutions on the word processor and to Vickie Hall who assisted; we also want to express heartfelt gratitude to Jane Isbell Haynes who gave many hours in tireless editing and critiquing the typescript in preparation for the publisher, and to Mrs. Roy Thurmond (Mary Ann) whose help in proof-reading was invaluable.

For the information which made possible the chapter on the Christ Methodist Day School, we express deep appreciation to Mrs. Charles McVean (Ella), Sam Drash, David Fox, and to Harry Johnson, Jr. who was on the first Board of Directors and aided in the founding and development of this quality school. We are also indebted to Harry Johnson for valuable information on the organization of the Christ Church Sunday School. He was the first Church School Superintendent and with the staff of officers and teachers, he overcame many obstacles in the path of a new and developing Church.

Regarding the chapter on the history of the United Methodist Women, we relied on information collected by Mrs. Mary Condra in a *History and Scrapbook*, and we relied on Mrs. Bea Crofford, Mrs. Eloise Mays, Mrs. Margaret Colby, Mrs. Rinne Ridolphi and all those who have been Presidents of the organization. We thank each and every one.

To each of you who are members of Christ United Methodist Church, we express appreciation, for without you there would be no Church about which to write a *History*. You are a very vital part of the worship, the outreach and the many activities that bless the lives of people around the world.

It is a great blessing to know that I have had the support of my family. Particularly do I thank my husband, Wayne Lamb, for his loving support and understanding of the task that involved many hours. He has always been a source of strength and encouragement.

We express appreciation to Reverend Earl Johnston for managing the publication of the manuscript.

To Dr. Maxie Dunnam, the Senior Minister, who was inspired to make the writing of the *History of Christ United Methodist Church* a part of our Thirtieth Anniversary Celebration, and who, with wisdom and counsel, gave us faith and confidence to attempt the task, we are eternally grateful.

Sincerely and with love,

Susan Ruby Breland Lamb

Introduction

History is a vision of God's creation — Man — on the move.
Every moment is a fresh beginning...

Because history is a vision of God's creation and every moment is a fresh beginning, we take time at intervals to review and record the deeds, activities and events of man on the move as they relate to us; therefore, on the Thirtieth Anniversary of Christ United Methodist Church, we have re-searched and recorded many of the highlights in the birth, growth and development of what has come to be one of Methodism's most dynamic, ministry-fulfilling Churches. In the beginning years, an excellent history of events in the development of Christ Church was recorded by Mrs. Elizabeth Templeton, Mrs. Rinne Ridolphi and Mrs. Ethel Whitenton. This early *History* was presented to the Church and is preserved in the Church Archives. Later Mrs. Frances L. Smith served as Historian and recorded and pre-served the history up to this date. In the Acknowledgements are recognition and appreciation to these persons for their "Labor of Love." Quoted from this early *History* are these ideas:

> History is the story of the thoughts and actions of men, words reporting the outgrowth of hopes, aspirations, struggles, failures and successes. History can never adequately record the depth of spirit in the men who have labored in love and hope and purpose; nor can the sacrifices involved ever be truly represented. Neither is history ever a complete story — as the years pass the story grows broader. It moves forward like a mighty wave on the ocean.

We are so fortunate to have six of the members of the organizational Steering Committee who are still members of Christ Church. Mr. Howard Davenport is living at NuCare Convalescent Center, Hot Springs, Arkansas. The other five are active members of Christ United Methodist Church: James H. Seabrook, Sr., E. C. Handorf, Samuel H. Mays, Fred Ridolphi and Lee B. McCormick. We asked these five persons to give us a statement on the "Highlight of their service on the Steering Committee."

E. C. Handorf was the secretary of the Steering Committee and kept the minutes of their meetings which met each Friday afternoon in Dr. J. E. Underwood's Office in the Falls Building, located west of Gerber's Depart-ment Store, facing Front Street, Memphis, Tennessee. Dr. Underwood was the District Superintendent for the Memphis District. E. C. Handorf made a valuable tape of the events of the Steering Committee and its work, and this tape is being preserved in the Church Archives for future reference. Originally, he was a member of First Methodist Church and had vivid recollections of their involvement in providing property and other resources for the beginning of the new Church. He reflected that being secretary of the Steering Committee was a very fulfilling experience as the eighteen members from the six sponsoring Churches engaged in full participation and came to have the feeling for each other of a warm and caring family. "The Holy Spirit was ever present, and when there were expressed varied opinions in the committee meetings, God's Will always prevailed."

If you have talked with Samuel H. Mays or have heard him speak, then you have learned that his being a part of the Steering Committee was an exciting time in his life. When the first Church Conference was held, he was elected the secretary and held this position for several years. He was the first Superintendent of the Youth Division and he and his wife, Eloise, gave hours of service in directing the youth in the Church School and guiding them in their many activities. Not only was the work of the Steering Committee a highlight in his life, but the results that were evidenced in that first Sunday of worship in the Plaza Theater, June 19, 1955, were also a peak experience as related by him:

> The Sunday had come! I had left home early to get to the Plaza to make sure everything was ready. For months we had called people, lined up teachers, enlisted ushers, worked out classroom space, ordered song books, literature, chairs and other supplies, all on faith. The hour was almost here, then it hit me! Suppose the people don't come. For me this was a very emotional moment, with tears in my eyes, I said, 'Lord, there isn't even time for one more phone call. It's all up to you'! And lo! what a glorious day it was.

Lee B. McCormick was an active participant in the life and plan of Christ Church from the very beginning. He served with James H. Seabrook, Sr. to negotiate the purchase of the property, at the corner of Poplar Avenue and Grove Park Road, with Hall Jones, who was the developer of the Laurelwood Shopping Center. This property was very valuable land being valued then at a quarter of a million dollars. Through their efforts it was sold to the Church for $95,000, and at that time, this was the largest price ever paid for property on which to build a church in the history of Methodism. Later Lee McCormick was elected to be the first Vice-Chairman of the Official Board and served on both the Architect Committee and the Finance Committee. He lists three things that stand out in his memory as he served on the Steering Committee:

1. The manner in which Dr. Charles W. Grant, the first pastor, was able to consolidate the members from many churches into one great Church. It would have been easy for cliques to have formed, but this never happened.
2. Not only did Christ Church pioneer in the largest price that was paid for church property, but later Church Extension made a gift to the project of $50,000, which up to that time was the largest amount that had been allocated to any project.
3. Above all was the faith that every member of the Steering Committee felt that a new church needed to be organized and built. No thought of failure ever existed.

Fred M. Ridolphi was a loyal supporter of the work of the Steering Committee from the beginning. He was elected to membership on the first Official Board, and at that time they had both a first and second Vice-Chairman. He was elected to be the second Vice-Chairman. He was also a member of the Welcome Committee who rendered such outstanding service under the leadership of C. R. McDaniel. He and his wife, Rinne, gave many hours in loving service to the building of this great Church; Mrs. Ridolphi was the second President of the Woman's Society of Christian Service. He recounts:

> It was a privilege to serve on the Steering Committee. I will always remember the wonderful spirit and talent of the members of the sponsoring churches. The cooperation and willingness of the members were outstanding. The growth of our Church has proven that the timing was right. We have been blessed in so many ways.

James H. Seabrook, Sr. was the Chairman of the Steering Committee and was also the first Chairman of the first Official Board; he gave many hours of dedicated service and leadership during the founding years. He has prepared an excellent "Summary History" of the work of the Steering Committee and of the many miracles that came to pass in the early life of Christ Church. He entitled the story of events *Christ United Methodist Church, A Venture In Faith*. This title, *Christ United Methodist Church, A Venture In Faith*, expresses so well the power of God and the spirit of faith and dedication on the part of the members that it has been chosen as the title for this *History*. Mr. Seabrook's "Summary History" has been placed in the Church Archives for future reference. He stated that when the Steering Committee began its work, there were no church, no members, no minister, no location, no building and no money in the bank. The Committee and others who were interested in building a new Church in East Memphis "waited upon the Lord." It was truly a "Venture in Faith." Other memorable cardinal events which he chronicled were the acquisition of the property and the tremendous response on the "Opening Sunday" in the Plaza Theater—they had prayed that they might have 300 persons present and lo! over 600 persons attended worship on that first Sunday. The Charter Membership of over 600 members was a first in Methodism. The sending of missionaries and the mothering of a new Church even before the erection of the first building—with the pledge to strive to always do as much for others as for themselves—was strikingly note-worthy. The naming of the Church was of great significance. Several names were suggested; for example, East Memphis Methodist Church or Poplar Street Methodist Church, but when the name Christ Methodist Church was presented, and it was explained that we wanted to say to the world that we wanted to be like Christ and to follow Him in His teaching when he said, "I came not to be ministered unto but to minister," then Christ Church was unanimously chosen as a name.

It is appropriate and essential that we quote from *A Venture in Faith* by James H. Seabrook, Sr. about the erection of the first building, Fellow-ship Hall:

> There was a feeling of great urgency to build our first permanent building. The cost at that time indicated a project involving $500,000. The banks were reluctant to make a temporary loan for such a project, since the new church was in its infancy and had no established record of raising money. However, the banks made the Church a proposal that if fifty of the members of the new Church would sign a note for $500,000, with limited liability of $10,000 each for the fifty members, they would make a temporary building loan of $500,000 with which to erect the building. A meeting of church members was held in The Chapel that had been erected on the property at 4400 Poplar. When the explana-tion was given and the call was made, fifty of our members went forward and signed the note for $500,000, each with $10,000 limited liability. This, too, was a wonderful 'Venture of Faith' and assured construction of Fellowship Hall.

At the Charge Conference of Christ United Methodist Church on January 8, 1985, these men, who were members of the organizational Steering Committee, were made honorary members of the Administrative Board in appreciation for their work thirty years ago in bringing Christ Church into being. The list included James H. Seabrook, Sr., E. C. Handorf, Samuel H. Mays, Lee B. McCormick, Fred M. Ridolphi, H. L. Davenport, Dr. W. J. Templeton and C. R. McDaniel.

In this Introduction are statements from five persons who had first-hand knowledge of the many miracles that came to pass in the "Venture in Faith"; therefore, this book is a story of God working through His people to build His kingdom on earth.

A Church is Born

Lean thine arm on the window sill of Heaven
And gaze upon thy God,
Then with the vision in thy heart
Turn strong to meet thy day.

— *anonymous*

The leaders of Methodism "turned strong to meet their day." In the early 1950's the leaders of Methodism became keenly aware of the moving of the population in the city of Memphis toward the east. They were concerned that we did not have churches in this area to meet the needs of a rapidly growing East Memphis. For many months Bishop W. T. Watkins and Dr. J. E. Underwood, District Superintendent of the Memphis District, worked on this concern. Finally it was concluded that they would ask six of the larger churches to sponsor the building of a large "Cathedral Type" Church to meet the needs of the fast growing East Memphis population. These six churches would be asked to name three members from their respective Official Boards to serve on a Steering Committee, which would meet regularly to study and formulate plans for an adequate new East Memphis Methodist Church.

The Steering Committee consisted of laymen from these six Memphis Churches:

First Methodist Church . . . . Howard L. Davenport
William E. Drenner
E. C. Handorf

Madison Heights Methodist Church . . . C. R. McDaniel
                                       Gerald T. Owens
                                       James H. Seabrook, Sr.
St. John's Methodist Church . . . . L. Palmer Brown, III
                                       Samuel H. Mays, Sr.
                                       John A. Parsons
St. Luke's Methodist Church . . . . Lee B. McCormick
                                       Edgar H. Tenent
                                       Dr. W. J. Templeton
Trinity Methodist Church . . . . H. W. Durham
                                       C. B. Johnston
                                       Fred M. Ridolphi
Union Avenue Methodist Church . . . . . L. G. Bone
                                       Clifford D. Pierce, Sr.
                                       A. C. Jones

The Steering Committee held its first meeting on December 10, 1954, with these members present: Howard L. Davenport, E. C. Handorf, L. G. Bone, John A. Parsons, Edgar H. Tenent and Gerald Owens. Dr. Underwood called the meeting to order and officers of the Steering Committee were elected:

Chairman . . . . James H. Seabrook, Sr.
Vice Chairman . . . . L. B. McCormick
Secretary . . . . E. C. Handorf
Treasurer . . . . John A. Parsons

During this meeting Dr. Underwood discussed the great need for an East Memphis Methodist Church to be located somewhere in the area of Poplar Avenue and Perkins Road. He also shared with the Committee the fact that property at 4370 Poplar Avenue, which had been purchased by First Methodist Church under the direction of Dr. W. C. Newman when they were considering moving their congregation out east, was adjacent to the Wallace property which might be secured to give more adequate room for the then new "Dream Church."

In the early discussions, many times there was a feeling of hopelessness and futility, but as the Steering Committee continued to work and pray, they felt that God was with them and that His Spirit was directing their thoughts and plans. The obstacles began to be removed and the dreams for the new Church began to evolve. The six sponsoring Churches along with their pastors had pledged full cooperation and support. The Steering Committee began to contact the members from these Churches who lived east of the Parkway to determine if there were sufficient interest among prospective members to move forward with the plans. The response was very encouraging, so the request was made to Bishop Watkins and Dr. Underwood that a pastor for the proposed Church be appointed at the Memphis Annual Conference meeting in June 1955. The Steering Committee emphasized the wish and need for a strong, spirit-filled minister, who also had administrative ability, to be selected for their pastor. They were gratified to learn that Dr. Charles W. Grant had been selected as the first Minister for the new Church-to-be. He had been the beloved Minister of Madison Heights Methodist Church and had come to the Memphis Conference from distinguished pastorates in both the Louisville and Kentucky Conferences.

Dr. Grant moved to Memphis in 1952 from Crescent Hill Methodist Church in Louisville, Kentucky, one of the three largest Methodist churches in Louisville at that time. He was born and reared in Mt. Vernon, Illinois, and was educated at Asbury College and Asbury Seminary in Wilmore, Kentucky. His Doctor of Divinity degree was conferred by Kentucky Wesleyan College, Owensboro, Kentucky. He is one of three brothers who became ministers; one brother was a missionary to China who died during the Sino-Japanese conflict and is buried in Shanghai.

Dr. and Mrs. Grant (Mary Anna) were dedicated and deeply committed to Christ and His Church including every facet of Kingdom building. No task was too great and no sacrifice too much; each task and sacrifice challenged the very best of their strength and devotion.

Someone has characterized Dr. Grant as a man with a remarkable sense of humor, a great and abiding love for the Bible, and a positive outlook toward life signified by the buoyancy of his step, by the brightness of the gleam in his eye, and by his cheerful and composed countenance. He knew the value of a long, quiet walk. He held a belief that there is still pioneering to be done in the Christian domain. After his appointment to be the Minister of Christ Church (which did not exist at that time), he was quoted as saying, "I want a church through which the love of God can be revealed to every man, woman, boy and girl who comes to worship with us. That is what is worth living for. I'm willing to die for the Church through which the Love of God flows." It has been said that he was virtually handpicked to lead this important new work. Dr. and Mrs. Grant were the parents of two children, Martha Ann (Mrs. William Likins) and David Lawrence.

There were many meetings of the Steering Committee as they moved forward with plans for an official beginning of the new Church after the Annual Conference in June 1955. The name for the new East Memphis Church was considered, and a number of names were suggested; among them was the name Christ Methodist Church. In the discussion it was affirmed that the name of Christ is above all other names, and it was concluded that it was the desire of the Steering Committee to honor His name and to hold

4

Dr. and Mrs. Charles W. Grant

it aloft as a constant example and challenge to the membership of the new Church. The Committee unanimously adopted the name of Christ Methodist Church.

Much research had been done in the Poplar-Perkins area in order to locate and acquire an appropriate and available site for the newly named Christ Methodist Church. On April 1, 1955, the Steering Committee purchased 6.4 acres of land situated at 4488 Poplar Avenue to be used for the permanent location, for $95,000, with a down-payment of $5,000. The property at 4370 Poplar Avenue owned by First Methodist Church was transferred to Christ Methodist Church through the District Church Extension Society. The price of this property was $32,800; First Methodist Church had paid $7,500, and Christ Methodist Church was to assume the balance of the indebtedness amounting to $25,300. This property afforded temporary quarters for a portion of the Sunday School, and for the business and administrative offices, as well as for a Chapel which was built later for Sunday evening worship services. The Church Extension Society also allocated $50,000 toward the new Church. Jesse Vineyard, an attorney and member of the Church, served ably as legal counsel from the very beginning of the Church. In the meantime, arrangements were made with Augustine Cianciola to rent the Plaza Theater for Sunday morning worship services for a rental fee of $100 per Sunday.

A notice was printed in the newspapers, and a letter was sent to interested and prospective members announcing the first Sunday Worship Service, to be held June 19, 1955, in the Plaza Theater, 3402 Poplar Avenue. Approximately 600 persons were present for this first worship service.

For many, going to church in a Theater was a unique experience, but God's presence was there in a remarkable way to dispel all distractions and warm the hearts of everyone. Someone expressed the uniqueness in this way:

> We were a congregation of Christians who had come from many churches with a unity of purpose—to build a new Church and fulfill a need in East Memphis . . . The Holy Spirit was present on that day and we left the meeting feeling as Paul must have felt as he went about the continent in his day establishing new churches.

The theme of Dr. Grant's message on this memorable Sunday was "The Birth of a Church." The message was so charged with hope and expectancy that many declared it to be the greatest day of their lives. These words of inspiration are from Dr. Grant's message:

> Today we find the challenge pointed to us to dare to believe as Abraham did. Progress, even in the Church, is seldom made

First worship service of Christ Methodist Church, June 19, 1955 at the Plaza Theatre, 3402 Poplar Avenue, Memphis. Dr. H.A. Butts, a Methodist Conference Evangelist, a tall man with white hair with hat in hand, stands left of center, and Arthur Barber, a blind Evangelistic Singer, stands to his left; Dr. Charles W. Grant stands slightly right of center, with his back to the camera, with his hand in his pocket; the tall man, with white hair, with back to the camera in the exact center is Howard L. Davenport.

without genuine pioneers—those so filled with faith that they move beyond the vision of the satisfied. God calls us to greatness of ambition for His kingdom, to dissatisfaction with the commonplace.

James H. Seabrook, Sr., Chairman of the Steering Committee, sent a letter to those who had expressed interest in becoming members of the new Church. In this letter everyone was invited to the worship service on June 26, 1955 at the Poplar-Plaza Theater at 10:30 a.m. where, "the District Superintendent, Dr. J. E. Underwood, will formally organize the new Christ Methodist Church. Dr. Grant's sermon will be entitled 'My New Church.' Those who present themselves for membership on this Sunday will be Charter Members of Christ Methodist Church." June 26, 1955, was a thrilling day in Methodism with 600 persons presenting themselves as Charter Members of the newly organized Christ Methodist Church. This was said to be the largest Charter Membership in the history of Methodism. The membership statistics were: (see names in Appendix XI)

From First Methodist, Dr. Roy D. Williams, Pastor 91
      Madison Heights, Rev. E. V. Underhill, Pastor 205
      St. John's, Dr. John L. Horton, Pastor 98
      St. Luke's, Dr. William C. Aden, Pastor 52
      Trinity, Dr. James D. Jenkins, Pastor 41
      Union Avenue, Dr. Wayne A. Lamb, Pastor 9
      Other Methodist Churches and otherwise . . . . <u>104</u>
               Total 600

Even though these Charter Members had held places of leadership in other Methodist Churches, they renewed their vows as they joined Christ Methodist Church on this organizational Sunday, and they rededicated themselves to do the task that was set before them.

The first Church School Superintendent was Harry A. Johnson, Jr., who spent countless hours buying and arranging the delivery of tables and chairs and other equipment for the Sunday School rooms. In the Plaza Area, there were the Theater rooms and also Britling's Cafeteria who opened their building for the Men's Bible Class. The Cottage at 4370 Poplar Avenue also had to be furnished with supplies. It was a thrill that more than 100 persons volunteered to be teachers or workers in the Church School.

For the first Sunday, careful preparation had been made for the first meeting of Church School, with a full staff of officers and teachers provided. The Nursery, Youth and Adult Divisions met at the Plaza Theater, and the Children's Division meeting was at the Cottage at 4370 Poplar Avenue. In

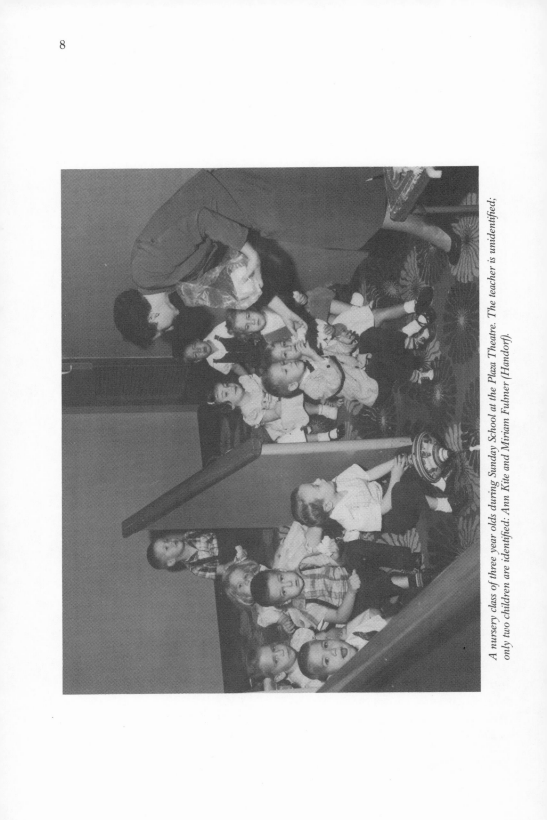

A nursery class of three year olds during Sunday School at the Plaza Theatre. The teacher is unidentified; only two children are identified: Ann Kite and Miriam Fulmer (Handorf).

Here is the church
and here is the steeple,
Open the door
and here are the people.

A Kindergarten class at Sunday School in "The Cottage," 1956. The teacher is Mrs. A.A. Sippel (Clarcy); children who can be identified are Melissa Mays (Robinson), Debbie Earls, William (Billy) Fones, Jesse Anderson, Jr., George Martin, Mary Jane Taylor.

the evening, the Youth Fellowship met in the Cottage, and also an evening worship service was held on the lawn at the 4370 Poplar address. Later a chapel known as "The Little Chapel" was built which met a vital need for other meetings and services.

The organizational committee for the Church School consisted of Harry A. Johnson, Jr., Chairman, Mrs. Charles McVean, Mrs. Richard Kite, Clarence Colby, J. B. Emerson, Mrs. A. A. Sippel, and Mr. and Mrs. Leland Helms. This committee proposed the following organization for beginning the Church School in the soon-to-be Christ Methodist Church:

Children's Division Superintendent	Mrs. Leland Helms
Nursery	Mrs. Charles McVean
Kindergarten	Mrs. A. A. Sippel
Primary	Mrs. Hugo Akin
Junior	Mrs. E. L. Carpenter
Youth Division Superintendent	Mrs. Sam Mays
Intermediate	Mrs. Richard Kite
Senior and Older Youth	Percy Whitenton
	Mrs. Percy Whitenton
Adult Division Superintendent	J. B. Emerson
Young Adult	Clarence Colby
Young Adult	Mrs. C. M. Henderson
Adult	John Parsons
Church School Secretaries	Clay Shelton
	Leland Helms

At the Christ Methodist Church Organizational Meeting held on June 26, 1955, in the Charge Conference presided over by the District Superintendent, Dr. J. E. Underwood, the following persons were elected as the first Trustees of Christ Methodist Church: James T. Canfield, Howard L. Davenport, C. R. McDaniel, John A. Parsons, Dr. W. J. Templeton and Edgar H. Tenent. Samuel H. Mays was elected secretary of the Charge Conference. At this same meeting the first Official Board was elected (see names in Appendix VI), and officers of the Official Board were elected at their first meeting: Chairman, James H. Seabrook, Sr.; First Vice Chairman, Lee McCormick; Second Vice Chairman, Fred Ridolphi; Secretary, Charles Tate; and Treasurer, John A. Parsons.

A committee to organize the Woman's Society of Christian Service in the new church was Mrs. Charles M. Henderson, Chairman, Mrs. Hugh Carey, Mrs. Percy Whitenton, Mrs. J. C. Ingram, Mrs. Thomas West, Mrs. Richard Taylor, Mrs. Oscar Crofford, Mrs. F. M. Ridolphi, Mrs. J. V. Thomas, and Mrs. H. C. Shelton. At the first meeting of the Woman's Society of Christian

"The Cottage" at 4370 Poplar avenue, 1955.

Service, officers were elected: President, Mrs. Percy Whitenton; Vice President, Mrs. Charles M. Henderson; Recording Secretary, Mrs. Jack Caskey; Treasurer, Mrs. Horace Harwell; and Assistant Treasurer, Mrs. W. K. Martak. Subsequently, women were elected Secretaries of various committees of work: Promotion, Mrs. Ned French; Missionary Education, Mrs. Clarence Colby; Christian Social Relations, Mrs. Fred Ridolphi; Student Work, Mrs. Sam Mays; Youth Work, Mrs. Charles Tate; Children's Work, Mrs. J. C. Ingram, Jr.; Spiritual Life, Mrs. W. J. Templeton; Literature and Publications, Mrs. Ray Drenner; Supplies, Mrs. Edgar Tenent; and Status of Women, Mrs. Jack Byrne. The following women accepted responsibility as Circle Leaders: Mrs. Howard Davenport, Mrs. Richard Taylor, Mrs. Russell Reeves, Mrs. Robert Holt, Mrs. J. T. Canfield, Mrs. Hugh Carey, Mrs. Ernest Felts, Mrs. E. R. Richmond, Mrs. Merle King, Mrs. John Parsons, and Mrs. D. K. Kelley. At this first meeting 157 women signed the Charter Book. Actually, the number of Charter Members was recorded later as 215 women in the organization that made missions around the world their primary concern.

Soon thereafter, the Wesleyan Service Guild was organized to meet the fellowship and service needs for business and professional women. Their first officers were: President, Mrs. Porter McClean; Vice President, Mrs. Haskell Glass; Secretary, Miss Zetta Walker; Treasurer, Miss Agnes Thomas; and Secretary of Promotion, Mrs. Floyd Dixon.

The Methodist Men also organized with a membership of 215. Their elected officers were: President, William Grumbles; First Vice President, John Whitsitt; Second Vice President, Horton Dubard; Secretary, W. K. Martak; and Treasurer, William Drenner. Howard L. Davenport was the first Church Lay Leader.

During these busy days with a multitude of details to discharge in the launching of a new Church, the members were not too occupied to organize a Boy Scout Troop, Number 241. The Scouts, along with many other groups, met in the Little Cottage at 4370 Poplar Avenue, until the first building could be built at 4488 Poplar Avenue. The Cottage was also the site of the temporary church offices, which in the beginning were completely void of furnishings, equipment or office supplies. Dr. Grant was overheard to say, "I wish I had a typewriter, but I am grateful that I have a lead pencil."

One of the appreciated services extended to Christ Church that was continued for a number of years was the contribution of printing the Sunday Bulletins by C. B. Johnston, owner of the C. B. Johnston Printing Company. He had been a valued member of the Steering Committee and a member of Trinity Methodist Church. One of the employees of this business designed the cover.

A Communion Service of Silver was presented to Christ Church by

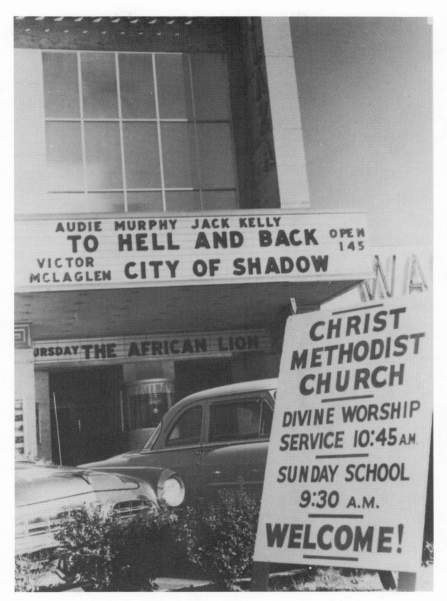

Christ Church sign juxtaposed to the movie marquee, 1955.

Mrs. Lillie C. Holley of Union Avenue Methodist Church. Following this gift H. C. Stroupe, Sr. built a Communion Altar Rail measuring thirty feet. Soon thereafter on July 17, 1955, the congregation celebrated their first Communion Service out under the stars at the 4370 Poplar address, known as the Little Cottage.

On August 16, 1955, a contract for architectural service was signed with Walk C. Jones, Jr. Committees were appointed to plan with the architect for the construction of the first unit of the building program of Christ Methodist Church at the 4488 Poplar location. When the plans were completed $500,000 was needed for this first building. There was no money, property or assets to provide security for the borrowing of this money, so fifty men underwrote the $500,000 loan. Almost four years later, it was indeed a happy day in May 1959 to witness a note-burning ceremony at a morning worship service. However, before the notes could be burned, funds had to be attained; the Officials of the Church employed Fred Alexander and Associates to conduct the fund-raising. A short-term campaign was conducted in September 1955, when $35,000 was pledged for the building of the Little Chapel at the 4370 Poplar address. Someone anonymously gave a beautiful brass cross to be placed behind the pulpit. This Chapel was completed in time for the congregation to celebrate their first Christmas Eve Communion, December 1955.

In 1956, the first three year building-fund pledge campaign was conducted, with a total of $376,000 pledged by members and friends.

The Parsonage Committee, under the Chairmanship of C. R. McDaniel, was unable to find a suitable location for the home of the Minister, so they arranged for Dr. and Mrs. Grant to live in an apartment in Magnolia Gardens in Windover Cove. However, in February 1956, the Commission on Finance with the recommendation of the Parsonage Committee arranged for the purchase of a home at 4227 Belle Meade Cove, in the Belle Meade Subdivision, to be the parsonage for the Minister and his family.

From the time of the organization of Christ Church in 1955 until January 1956, Jesse Anderson and Moody Cunningham served without salary as Directors of the Choir, and Mrs. Herbert Dunkman donated her services as Organist. The weekly choir rehearsals were held in Mrs. Dunkman's home. After the beginning of the new year, Dr. George Muns was employed as part-time Choir Director and Mrs. Byron Hudson was chosen as Organist. Mrs. Earle Billings looked after the office on a part-time basis. At this time Mrs. Rosaline Ford was employed as the first Financial Secretary.

In the weeks and months that followed there were many inconveniences and hardships that were related to beginning a new church. However, Dr. Grant and the congregation gave little attention to hinderances, and they kept their eyes fixed on the goal of their consuming desire to build a great Methodist Church that would not only be a beacon of love and redemption here in the city of Memphis but also a monument to God's power and glory to the ends of the world. They were inspired and challenged as were the people of Nehemiah's day when they were rebuilding the walls of Jerusalem, "for the people had a mind to work." Someone expressed it this way, "As we progressed, the tasks seemed lighter, and we had great joy in performing them."

The spirit of the membership at the end of our first year is perhaps best expressed with an excerpt from a letter written to Bishop Watkins by the Pastoral Relations Committee, dated March 20, 1956:

> Our membership is enthusiastic and working, and we believe that God has been directing our efforts and has given us results and blessings far beyond our hopes and dreams. One of the greatest blessings has been the wise, consecrated ministry of our beloved minister, Dr. Charles W. Grant, who has given us leadership in all fields that could not be surpassed. We want to express our deep appreciation to our Bishop and our District Superintendent for their vision, sympathetic understanding and cooperation. As we build with brick and stone, we dedicate ourselves and our Church to spiritual values — to the promotion of the Methodist Church — to the extension and development of the Kingdom — to the salvation of men's souls — to the conquest of the world for our Lord and Saviour, Jesus Christ.

A significant occasion on Easter Sunday, April 1, 1956, was the ground-breaking ceremony for the first building to be erected on the property at 4488 Poplar Avenue. Bishop Watkins was unable to be present, so the service was conducted by the District Superintendent, Dr. J. E. Underwood. Others who assisted in this event were Dr. Grant, James H. Seabrook, Sr., John A. Parsons, and Howard Davenport. This first unit to be built was designed to be an educational building with a large Fellowship Hall, seating 600 people, that would serve both for a sanctuary and a dining hall for church dinners. The first new building would also contain church offices, Sunday School rooms and other facilities. The planned cost was approximately $378,000 with about $70,000 worth of equipment.

A little more than a year after the new Church began its meetings and services in the Plaza Theater on Poplar Avenue in the Plaza area and in the Cottage and in the Little Chapel at 4370 Poplar Avenue, the Memphis *Commercial Appeal* carried pictures and a story on the front page of one of the newspaper sections entitled, "Growing Pains Bring Problems To The New Church." The narrative explained how the Sunday School teachers and workers were trying to take care of more than 800 children and adults.

Groundbreaking ceremony for the first building, the Fellowship Hall, Easter Sunday, April 1, 1956. Left to right, James H. Seabrook, Sr., Dr. J.E. Underwood, John Parsons, Howard Davenport, Dr. Charles W. Grant, and Dr. James Jenkins behind Dr. Grant.

Someone remarked that the great number of children in the classes reminded them of the "Old lady who lived in a shoe—she had so many children she didn't know what to do." Pictures illustrated the crowded quarters.

The history of the first year would not be complete without some of the statistics which were a part of the Report for Annual Conference 1956:

Total Membership 876
Church School Membership 781
Woman's Society of Christian Service 248
Methodist Men's Club 221
Total Budget $193,422

A summary of the first year in the life of Christ Methodist Church is visible in the quote from a letter written by Dr. Grant to the Fourth Quarterly Conference:

When all the facts and figures are in, the achievements of Christ Methodist Church for the first year will far exceed the highest hopes of the most ambitious. Momentarily we are awaiting specifications from the Architect and shortly thereafter contracts will be let and actual construction on one of our buildings will begin. These are anxious days for the leadership of this church.

There are many emphases in Christ Methodist Church: Stewardship, Missions, Youth, Education, Music, Evangelism, Service, and of necessity, Building, but the primary emphasis and the one in which we expect to intensify our efforts is to seek first the Kingdom of God and His righteousness. Laymen and minister alike feel that we must have a spiritual church—a church that will minister to the hearts of men and women of this area—a pulpit that will send forth "no uncertain sound," declaring to all the whole gospel of full salvation, the power of God to save unto the uttermost by Jesus Christ our Lord. It is for this reason that Christ Methodist Church is to be built. It is to this high position that we daily rededicate ourselves as pastor and people. Surely the coming of Christ Methodist Church into our lives has brought inestimable blessings.

From the very beginning, much of the publicity for Christ Methodist Church contained the theme, "Methodism's Contemporary Church With A Vital Spiritual Thrust."

Faith at Work

And ye shall be witnesses unto me both in Jerusalem, and in all Judea,
and in Samaria, and unto the uttermost part of the earth.

— Acts 1:8 (KJV)

During the next several years many unusual adventures were attempted
and noteworthy ministries were launched. Even though Christ Church was
just getting started and did not have its own buildings, we pledged a total of
$24,000 to sponsor Scenic Hills Methodist Church which was being organized
in Frayser, Tennessee. This amount was an increase over our usual Conference askings for Church Extension, and the request included the privilege
of our directing the funds to this new work.

Another result of great faith on the part of the Pastor, Dr. Charles Grant,
the Commission on Missions, and the Congregation, was the feeling of
urgency to follow our Lord's command when he said, "Seek ye first the
kingdom of God . . ."; therefore, in August 1956, a program was inaugurated
to support two medical missionaries.

William E. Drenner, Chairman of the Commission on Missions, made a
trip to New York and visited the office of the Board of Missions and learned
that it might be possible for Christ Church to assume the support of Dr. and
Mrs. Harold Brewster. Dr. Brewster was serving at that time as head of the
Medical Section of the World Division of the Board of Missions. This support would make it possible for Dr. and Mrs. Brewster to go to Sarawak,
Borneo, where they would establish Christ Hospital at Kapit. After thorough
discussion, it was decided that the Church would accept the challenge of
assuming full support of the two missionaries, which at that time amounted

to $4,800 per year. The missionary spirit unmistakably caught fire in the congregation; this program was sponsored with individual pledges and gifts for the support of the missionaries. It was opportune and fortunate that Dr. and Mrs. Brewster were able to visit our Church before leaving for Borneo. This visit, together with the exchange of letters that followed in the succeeding months, strengthened the bond between Christ Church in Memphis and Christ Hospital in Kapit, Sarawak.

In 1956, Reverend B. L. Gaddie was appointed as our first Associate Minister. After he and his family remained with us a year, he was appointed Pastor, in 1957, of the new Scenic Hills Methodist Church on Scenic Highway in Frayser, Tennessee. Others who joined our staff were: Robert L. Sanders, Jr., on September 1, 1957, as Director of the Sanctuary Choir; Barry DeZonia, in the fall of 1957 to serve as Assistant Administrator; and Mrs. P. B. Whitenton, employed on January 1, 1958, as our first Parish Visitor. In February 1958, Mrs. Sam Dunn was employed as the first Hostess-Dietician, and the Fellowship Dinners at the Church were initiated.

The Laying of the Cornerstone for the new Fellowship Hall Building occurred on August 25, 1957 with Dr. Grant officiating and the following officials participating: Howard Davenport, E. C. Handorf, Dr. Howard Boone, William Drenner, Jeans Pattinson, Mrs. Clarence Colby, John A. Parsons and James H. Seabrook, Sr. Precious and valuable documents, as well as many favorite scriptures of members of the congregation, were placed in the metal box to be preserved in the Cornerstone. Fellowship Hall Building was opened on March 1, 1958; it contained a temporary sanctuary-social hall combination, office areas, a temporary choir room, classrooms for the Junior Department and an all-steel kitchen. Preceding the first worship service to be held in Fellowship Hall Sanctuary, March 2, 1958, Dr. Grant had announced that the Sanctuary would be open for prayer on Saturday evening, March 1, and he invited the members to come to pray at the altar as long as they would like. It was his desire that the building be saturated with prayer and the Word of God. The lights were turned low and the lighted cross was the central and predominant illumination.

In the Sunday worship service the next morning, held on March 2, Dr. Grant's sermon was aglow with the Holy Spirit. He proclaimed:

Let this be a day of participation, every member participating in Christ's work; let it be a day of dedication, every member dedicating his all to Christ; let this be a day of anticipation, with high hopes for the future; let this be a day of ascription, giving unto God all the glory for His magnificent achievements.

The report made to Annual Conference in Jackson, Tennessee, June 18, 1958, asserted that Christ Methodist Church had assumed full responsibility in all local, district, conference and world-wide ministries. In support of Wesley House, Church Extension, and Borneo, Christ Church had gone beyond the Conference askings. The Church had experienced phenomenal growth and God had seemed to add his signal blessings.

After serving as our missionaries to Borneo, Dr. and Mrs. Brewster returned to the United States. The Church was in need of a replacement, and it was the good fortune of Christ Church to be able to give full support to Dr. and Mrs. Loreto Crisologo and their son, Peter. When the Brewsters came home in September 1958, they visited Christ Church and related many experiences of their work in Borneo, each inspirational to the congregation.

About this time we were privileged to have Dr. Frank C. Laubach, the great apostle of literacy, visit our Church and tell of the wonderful program of "Each One Teach One." As he spoke as a Guest Minister, he told how the program had enabled 100,000,000 in 267 languages and dialects living in ninety-four countries to become literate.

The Commission on Education under the Chairmanship of Harry A. Johnson, Jr. initiated and sponsored a Day School Kindergarten, beginning in September 1958, with an enrollment of seventy-five pupils. By the end of the year under the able leadership of Mrs. Charles A. McVean, it was appraised as an overwhelming success. An addendum to this story of continued success and ministry is written in a separate chapter about the Christ Methodist Day School.

Because of continued growth and splendid church attendance, the Official Board voted in October 1958 to provide two morning worship services — one at 8:30 a.m. and the other at 10:45 a.m., making it possible for the Church to accommodate a larger congregation in a more comfortable and worshipful manner.

We had been without an Associate Minister from the time of Conference in June until November 1958 when Reverend Marshall R. Morris came to Christ Church from the Julia Gay Memorial Methodist Church in Chicago, Illinois, where he had been serving while he was working on his Bachelor of Divinity degree at Garrett Theological Seminary. Also in November 1958, two persons were added to the staff in the Music Department: Miss Julia Garner became Assistant Organist and Mrs. Delores Kinsolving began volunteer direction of the Youth Choir.

The Christmas Season of 1958 was especially sustentative because the Church had the first Christmas Eve "silent come and go" Holy Communion from 5:00 p.m. to 7:00 p.m. On December 21, 1958, a beautiful vesper service with traditional Christmas music was held in the Fellowship Hall Sanctuary. The true spirit of Christmas is infinitely more than the aroma of plum pudding, the sight of children's stockings hung on the mantel and beautifully wrapped packages. The Christmas story and its hope may be expressed in one word, "Emmanuel"—God with us!

At the Quarterly Conference in January 1959, Edward Horton, a student in Candler School of Theology, Emory University, Atlanta, Georgia, was recommended for Local Preacher's License.

It seems almost incredible that in January 1959, Christ Methodist Church was ready to launch the campaign to raise funds and begin construction of their second unit—a building consisting mostly of classrooms. Again Fred Alexander was engaged to lead the financial campaign. The goal was established to obtain pledges amounting to $600,000 to be paid over a three year period. The campaign closed with a total of $621,000 pledged.

Early in 1959, an Award of Merit from the American Institute of Architects for the Gulf States Region and the Award of Merit from the Church Architectural Guild of America was presented to Walk Jones, Jr., Architect, for architectural achievement in the design and plans of the Fellowship Hall Building.

The size of the church began to increase. Mrs. Avis D. Allen became Financial Secretary in January 1959, and Noel Gilbert was employed as violinist and was designated to assist the Youth Choirs on Sunday night. Mrs. Tom Ragland (Glenn) served as Membership Secretary for a number of years; she always had an up-to-date report on the membership statistics, and she also prepared the bulletins. At this time, office space was limited and she referred to working part of the time in a closet.

During Holy Week in 1959, the Sanctuary Choir presented "The Crucifixion" by Sir John Stainer for the Maundy Thursday Service.

As we approached the end of the 1959 Conference year, a formal ceremony of note-burning took place in May. This document contained the signatures of the fifty men who had guaranteed in 1955 the loan of $500,000 on the first unit of the Church, the Fellowship Hall Building.

The Pastor's Report which was presented to Annual Conference in 1959, contained these statistics:

Total Membership 1413
Church School Membership 1198
Woman's Society of Christian Service 401
Methodist Men's Club 115

During the summer of 1959, Christ Church had reached such heights and made such progress that it was thought advisable to send two other missionaries into another field of service. Through research on the part of the Commission on Missions under the Chairmanship of George Atkinson,

Mr. and Mrs. Edward Heyer were selected to serve in Southern Rhodesia, Africa. Again we pledged to undergird their full support, making a total of four missionaries that the congregation was completely financing. The Heyer's work was in the fields of education and agriculture in this vital geographical area of Africa.

In the November 15, 1959 church bulletin, Dr. Grant challenged the congregation further:

> Our history, while brief—4½ years—has been glorious. Our future is challenging and stimulating. What great things God can do for us and through us if we will allow Him. The way to make the future great with no regrets is to dedicate the present, its every moment and movement to Him.

Imagine the great joy when on December 20, 1959 the cornerstone for the second unit of the Church Plant was laid. The Building Committee, composed of Al W. Lenz, Chairman, Ed Richmond, Sr., Gil Avery, James Canfield, Earl Montgomery, and Dennis Earles, Sr., met with the Architect, Walk C. Jones, Jr., and recommended that this second building be named the Charles W. Grant Building. Over the protest of Dr. Grant, this motion was adopted. The recommendation was then carried to the Official Board and was unanimously adopted. Dr. Grant's response was gracious:

> As pastor I wish to express my sincere appreciation to the official members for this gracious and undeserved action. I do not deserve it. It is a thrilling joy to be the pastor of such a great, far-sighted and daring, dedicated group. What success the Church may have had or may now be experiencing in any realm, whether spiritual or material, is due largely to two things: first, the blessings of God, which we all cherish; and second, the wonderful lay leadership and spirit of cooperation.

At a meeting in Knoxville, Tennessee at the beginning of the New Year 1960, the "Decade of Prayer" was ushered in. The purpose was for every Methodist to dedicate himself or herself to the task of total prayer for total evangelism for the total Church during the Decade of Prayer, 1960-1970. The Pastor, Dr. Grant, preached a series of messages on prayer and then the laity was given an opportunity to sign a covenant to be "Prayer Partners." The power of God's grace flowed through the congregation and great and awe-inspiring things happened almost daily. Just at this time our first revival was planned. Reverend Joseph T. Edwards of Detroit, Michigan, was chosen to lead us in the services from February 7 to February 12, 1960.

On Sunday, February 14, 1960, the Church School occupied for the first time the new Charles W. Grant Building. It was consecrated by Bishop Marvin Franklin, presiding Bishop of the Memphis Conference. Shortly thereafter the property at 4370 Poplar Avenue with the Cottage and the Little Chapel on it, which had served so well in those beginning years, was sold to Silver Homes Incorporated, for the amount of $85,000. Previous payments of notes on this property, amounting to $30,000, had been paid to Leader Federal Savings and Loan Association, Memphis.

It was in 1960 that Miss Joanne Brattain joined our staff as our first Director of Religious Education and Mrs. Robert L. Sanders, Jr. was employed as Assistant Organist.

We were saddened in June of 1960 by the death of our former District Superintendent, Dr. J. E. Underwood. He will be remembered for the magnificent leadership he gave in the organization of this Church. A fitting Memorial Window was placed in the Sanctuary in his memory.

Pressing Toward the High Calling

I press toward the mark for the prize of the high calling of God in Christ Jesus.

—Philemon 3:14 (KJV)

Upon entering the decade of the nineteen hundred and sixties, wonderful things continued to happen in the life of Christ Methodist Church to bless not only the church members but also other people around the world with whom there was a sharing of Christ and His love. Great emphasis was placed on faith in God and charity toward all men.

In 1961, Dr. Grant received an invitation to participate in a preaching mission to Korea, which included important preaching, teaching and counseling ministries at Ewha Woman's University in Seoul. The church encouraged Dr. and Mrs. Grant to accept this invitation and were very supportive in making the necessary arrangements. It was exciting to know that they would have an opportunity to visit Christ Hospital in Sarawak, Borneo to which the Church had been giving support. They were also privileged to visit other mission work in Hong Kong, Japan, Singapore and Sibu. At the conclusion of the evangelistic services in Korea, 1,289 persons were baptized as accepting Christ into their lives. The Church received a letter of deep appreciation from the late Dr. Helen Kim, thanking the church for sharing Dr. and Mrs. Grant with the students of Ewha Woman's University during these important and blessed days.

In February 1961, the Church Library was opened. Many contributions were made to this ministry of information and inspiration. Volumes were given in honor and in memory of loved ones and friends.

On Easter Sunday 1961, William Edward Horton was presented a local preacher's license by Dr. Grant. This made Reverend Horton the first person to enter the ministry from Christ Church. The records show that Ed Horton joined Christ Church July 5, 1955 and became a member of the Memphis Annual Conference June 17, 1961.

This was the year that the Men's Prayer Breakfast was organized; the date was October 13, 1961. To this day, this Prayer Group is a tower of strength. This was also the year when thirty-two men became Charter Members of the Fisherman's Club, pledging their loyalty to put forth every effort to win as many souls as possible to Christ and His church.

It was also in 1961 that the Official Board voted to instruct the ushers to seat—at their discretion—anyone who came to worship.

The weeks and months seemed to abound with the blessings of God. The membership continued to grow and already there were two fine buildings in which to worship and work. Now the plans were ready to launch the third building-funds campaign and build the long awaited Sanctuary. This work would begin in February 1962 with high enthusiasm which helped to bring the construction to an early and successful conclusion.

Our first Maundy Thursday Service was a part of the Holy Week observance which followed closely our revival services which had been held the early part of April 1962, with Dr. Thorton Fowler of McKendree Methodist Church in Nashville, Tennessee leading that meeting.

About this time the Trustees reported to the Quarterly Conference in 1962, the purchase of the land and two white clapboard residences at 4448 Poplar Avenue and 4468 Poplar Avenue. The Church had an immediate need for this property, using the house at 4448 Poplar Avenue for the parsonage for the Associate Minister and the other residence at 4468 Poplar Avenue for a Youth Center. These houses also served another purpose, that of keeping faith with the neighborhood, in providing a kind of buffer between residential and commercial areas.

In addition to providing a house for our Youth Activities, the Church was able to employ for the months of June, July, and August 1962, Reverend David Robertson, a graduate of Yale and a student at Perkins School of Theology at Southern Methodist University, Dallas, Texas.

Another beautiful occasion happened when twenty-two boys from Boys' Town presented themselves for membership in Christ Church and twenty-two of the men of the Church came forward and stood with them to sponsor them and be a kind of "Spiritual Father" to them.

The musical programs of the Church were always of great inspiration, and every member learned to look forward to special occasions like Christmas when the Sanctuary Choir, under the leadership of Mr. Robert L. Sanders, Jr. and Mrs. Byron Hudson at the organ, presented original music and drama for these services. The choir was dedicated to giving of themselves for practice and service. In 1962, Mrs. John Hendricks joined the staff as Director of Children and Youth Choirs.

Dr. and Mrs. Crisologo, our missionaries from Borneo, were in the United States on a Sabbatical leave and visited at the Thanksgiving Season, 1962, speaking at both the morning and evening worship services on Sunday. They also met with the diverse Sunday School classes including the children and youth of the Church. Each time missionaries come to visit, it is thrilling to hear of their work and to know that Christ Church is helping spread the Gospel of Christ in distant lands.

The New Year 1963 began with Dr. Grant's presenting at a worship service the license to preach to William Cobb, son of Mr. and Mrs. C. H. Cobb.

Another exciting contract was signed on May 6, 1963 with F. T. Thayer, General Contractor, for the construction of the Christ Church Sanctuary for the sum of $834,805, to be built in 370 working days. This contract was signed by E. R. Richmond, Sr., Chairman of the Architect and Building Committee, Edgar Tenent, Chairman of the Official Board and James H. Seabrook, Sr., Chairman of the Trustees. The plans were prepared by two architectural firms laboring and collaborating together: James B. Adams, Architect, and Thorn, Howe, Stratton and Strong, Associated Architects.

On the next Sunday, May 12, 1963, following the morning worship, the Sanctuary ground-breaking service was held. The congregation assembled on the southeast corner of the property at 4488 Poplar Avenue for the ceremony and they were joined by friends from all over the city; Mayor Henry Loeb was present, and Mr. F. T. Thayer, Jr., General Contractor, was also there. The event was televised by WMCT-Television Station. The participants in the ground-breaking used gold spades to turn the soil. On this memorable occasion, it was noted that among the crowd, representatives were present from Protestant, Catholic and Jewish faiths.

The "Aldersgate Commemoration" was observed in 1963 with the youth presenting a drama entitled, "Awakening at Aldersgate," supported with music by the Church Choir. Dr. J. Manning Potts, editor of *The Upper Room*, was the guest speaker for this celebration.

Several interesting events took place at the time of Annual Conference, June 1963. William H. Crump was added to the staff as a full time Director of Christian Education. Reverend Howard W. Rash was appointed as an Associate Minister. He and his wife, Mary, are the parents of two children, Carolyn and Ken.

A message from Dr. Grant further emphasized the commitment to missions that Christ Methodist Church stressed:

I am standing here in one place, and yet by the miracle of missions my feet are treading the path of mercy around the world in forty countries. I have two unskilled hands and yet by the miracle of missions these hands are performing delicate operations in Christ's Hospital in Sarawak. I can speak only one language and yet by the miracle of missions I am telling the story of Jesus Christ in a hundred languages around the world... In addition to this we are concentrating on three areas: Our medical missionaries, Dr. and Mrs. Loreto L. Crisologo, serve hundreds of people in Kapit, Sarawak and Borneo; our educational missionaries, Reverend and Mrs. E. L. Heyer, teach hundreds of people in Southern Rhodesia; and our newest missionaries, Reverend and Mrs. James L. Gravely, III (with daughter, Beth) serve in rural Brazil.

On April 24, 1964, a Ministerial Recruitment Library was presented to the Church at the Sunday morning worship service, by William E. Drenner, President of the Denton County National Bank of Denton, Texas, in memory of his father, Ray Drenner, and in honor of his mother, Fern Ruth. The value of the library was placed at $900, and it will be available for all ministers, particularly young ministerial students who may want to explore the field and validate their call of God to preach. This was a beautiful tribute to Mr. and Mrs. Drenner, both of whom had meant so much to the life and history of Christ Church; he was very active on the Church organizational committees and Mrs. Drenner was the Church Dietician for a number of years and rendered untiring and efficient service.

On October 18, 1964, the cornerstone of the Sanctuary was laid. The congregation was invited at the worship service to write sentence prayers, favorite scriptures or commitments to be collected by the ushers and placed in the box and sealed in the cornerstone. The new Sanctuary was opened for worship on November 1, 1964. It was a place of beauty and a joy to behold. The net membership of the Church had grown to 1,983. The Sanctuary was built to seat 1,510, but the ushers used many chairs on this first Sunday and they estimated the crowd to be 1,750. On this very special Sunday, eighteen persons united with the Church, increasing the number of the total membership to 2,001. The opening of the new Sanctuary eliminated the need for two Sunday morning worship services. One of the members who wished to remain anonymous gave the Pew Bibles which are used in the Sanctuary. In the Memorial Plaque Book is a listing of the memorials, such as the stained glass windows, the Communion Table, pews and other special gifts.

Music makes such an inestimable contribution to the worship services, and for a church, there is perhaps no finer instrument than the pipe organ. At this first Sunday service on November 1, 1964, Mrs. Byron Hudson was at

The Sanctuary in progress in July 1963 looking toward Poplar Avenue from the Altar-to-be.

The laying of the Sanctuary cornerstone ceremony on October 18, 1964. Left to right: R. Keith Weisinger, Everett C. Handorf, Reverend Howard W. Rush, Dr. Charles W. Grant, Gloria Hendrix.

the console of the organ and Mrs. John Hendricks assisted with sweet music from the violin. The new organ is one of the finest instruments in Memphis. It was built by M. P. Moler Incorporated of Hagerstown, Maryland, and includes fifty-five ranks of pipes with electro-pneumatic action and a movable console. It was installed in its present position in 1964. The antiphonal division is located in the balcony, but all other pipes are located above and on both sides of the chancel area. The Schulmerick Carillon was installed in 1969 and was a gift from Kemmons Wilson, founder of Holiday Inns, and his family, as a memorial to Mr. Wilson's mother, Ruby L. (Doll) Wilson. It is known as the "Americana" carillon. It is actually an electro-mechanical bell in which tiny, bronze rods of bell metal are struck by tiny hammers or "clappers" to produce the tones of either Flemish-tuned or English-tuned bells. The carillon can be played from the keyboard of the organ console, and selector switches permit the bells to be heard from the Carillon tower or heard exclusively inside the Sanctuary. At Christmas 1975, Mr. and Mrs. Jack Renshaw donated the money to cover the purchase price of the organ and it was dedicated "To the Glory of God" and to the spiritual and musical enrichment of mankind in honor of their children, Dorothy Cecile and Robert Jarrett.

Downstairs in the Sanctuary building, a lovely chapel was built to be used for smaller services than those in the larger Sanctuary; Mr. and Mrs. Russell E. Reeves, Sr. gave the chapel in memory of their son, First Lieutenant Russell E. Reeves, Jr., an airplane bomber-pilot stationed on Guam who was killed in the Pacific Theater in World War II.

During the Thanksgiving Season of 1964, it was a joy for the congregation to share the beauty and reverence of the Sanctuary with other Methodist churches throughout the city as they joined in a Community Thanksgiving Service.

Christmas 1964 was celebrated, as always, with a number of special events. A dramatic Christmas Pageant was presented by the Youth of the Church, in addition to an outstanding Cantata, "The King of Kings" by Prothroe, presented by both the Chancel and Youth Choirs. Reverend Heyer, our missionary from Southern Rhodesia, returned to the United States on furlough and visited on December 13. He spoke to a number of groups in the Church telling about his work in that land in Africa. On December 27, Bishop Homer Ellis Finger visited the church and preached from the subject, "God's Idea of the Church." According to the Methodist Church *Book of Discipline*, a church cannot be dedicated until it is free of debt; however, a Consecration Service is appropriate and in order at any time. Therefore at the conclusion of the sermon by Bishop Finger, the Chairman of the Architect and Building Committee, Ed R. Richmond, Sr., and James H. Seabrook, Sr., President of the Board of Trustees, made the presentation of the Sanctuary to Bishop Finger. The Bishop in turn accepted the presentation and declared "... that the Church be open for the worship of God and the service of men."

The year 1965 was our Anniversary Year, completing the first decade in the life and service of Christ Methodist Church. A change in our music ministry took place early in this year. Mr. and Mrs. Robert Sanders and Mrs. John Hendricks who had given such splendid service on a part-time basis were retiring from this responsibility. The Music Committee and the Official Board decided to employ a full time Minister of Music who would devote himself to a full choir program including multiple choirs. Paul Schultz joined the staff, coming to Memphis after serving more than twelve years at First Presbyterian Church of Tulsa, Oklahoma. During the year Schultz organized and trained four choirs in addition to the Chancel Choir:

> The Angelus Choir . . . . Second and Third Grade Children
> Carol Choir . . . . Fourth, Fifth and Sixth Grade Girls
> David Boy Choir . . . . Fourth, Fifth and Sixth Grade Boys
> Wesley-Oxford Choir . . . . . Seventh to Twelfth Grade Youth

These choirs presented many beautiful programs for special occasions, specifically at Easter and Christmas.

The Memphis Chapter of the American Guild of Organists presented an organ recital *beatae memoriae* in the Sanctuary on the magnificent new organ, February 8, 1965 at 8:15 p.m. In addition to Mrs. Byron Hudson, the Church Organist, Richard White, celebrated Organist and Choir-Master of St. John's Episcopal Church, Memphis, Tennessee was a guest artist; Mrs. Gordon Hollingsworth, well-known in Memphis music circles, also rendered outstanding music.

On May 30, 1965 at 7:30 p.m. in the Sanctuary, the choirs combined, making a total of 184 voices, in presenting the first "Spring Festival of Choirs." Paul Schultz directed; the choirs performed both separately and together in a magnificent evening of music. After years of faithful service, Mrs. Byron Hudson resigned in 1965 as Organist and Kenneth W. Stellwagon was employed to succeed her. Stellwagon rendered an organ concert as a memorial to the late Dr. Albert Schweitzer, world renowned authority on Bach, celebrated organist and Christian missionary.

On June 8-11, 1965, the Twenty-seventh Session of the Memphis Annual Conference was held at Christ Church. The sessions were filled with worship, business, fellowship and entertainment. Bishop Homer Ellis Finger was the presiding officer and Dr. J. Wallace Hamilton was the inspirational preacher for these special days. The new Methodist Hymnal was introduced during these sessions. An especial highlight of the Annual Conference was the unveiling of the portrait of Dr. Charles W. Grant in the Educational Building that bears his name. When the appointments were read, Dr. Grant and Reverend Howard W. Rash were returned to Christ Church as Ministers.

In addition to Dr. Hamilton, who was the preacher for Annual Conference, we had other distinguished ministers to visit Christ Church for special services. Dr. Ralph W. Sockman, Dean of National Radio Preachers and Minister and Pastor of Christ Methodist Church in New York City, led us in five unforgettable services. Dr. Harry Denman, Executive Secretary of the Board of Evangelism, led us in some noteworthy days of Evangelism and Dr. Fred Pfisterer, Pastor of Fourth Avenue Methodist Church in Louisville, Kentucky, preached and guided us through a series of significant revival services.

Both the Memphis *Commercial Appeal* and the Memphis *Press-Scimitar* carried a news story with glowing accounts of the Anniversary Service in June 1965 that celebrated ten years of service for the new Christ Methodist Church:

> Ceiling-high panels of stained glass pageantry framed a giant cross suspended over a milky white marble altar, as a congregation of about 2,100 celebrated their tenth anniversary.
>
> Christ Methodist Church at Poplar and Grove Park met for the first time ten years ago in the Plaza Theater. About 600 persons became charter members at that meeting. Yesterday 400 of the original congregation, with lapel ribbons, were mixed with hundreds more as one of the city's fastest growing Methodist congregations briefly reviewed its past and listened to a call for dedication to the future.

The congregation that once met in a rented Theater Hall for 140 Sundays under a movie marquee, was now in a Sanctuary with a tall fluted spire and facilities valued at 2.5 million dollars. In Dr. Grant's sermon that day, he told the congregation, "The past says to the present, that devotion to Christ pays big dividends." God's presence was made more real as ten persons presented themselves for membership in the Church at this historic Tenth Anniversary Service. Not only has Christ Church been a praying church but, as stressed from the beginning, it was to be a missionary church. A communication from the treasurer of the World Division of the Board of Missions, specified that Christ Methodist Church ranked seventh in "Advance Special Giving" among all the churches in America. This was significant for it meant that only six other churches were giving more to the Advance Program than Christ Church. The amount for this particular year of 1965 amounted to $22,500.

Someone has said that Dr. Grant always prepared the congregation for deeper consecration in worship. From the very inception of Christ Methodist Church, Dr. Grant had set the mood for the Sunday morning worship with this invitation to prayer:

> Lean thine arm on the window sill of Heaven
> And gaze upon thy God,
> Then with the vision in thy heart
> Turn strong to meet thy day.

By this graphic metaphor, this invitation to prayer was so indelibly impressed on all the members, that even a child was prompted to say to her mother upon seeing the tester above the pulpit when the Sanctuary was completed: "Look, Mother, there's Dr. Grant's window sill to Heaven."

To Serve the Present Age

I am the light of the world: he that followeth me shall not walk in darkness, but shall have the light of life.

—John 8:12 (KJV)

In Christ Church, there has been remarkable growth in membership and financial goals, and now in looking to the future, the Church is ready to concentrate on Evangelism and growth in Spiritual Life and combat the waves of secularism, futility and meaninglessness of life that seem to prevail in the world. Dr. Grant stressed that the Church is a community of believers, recognizing that we do not find the answers to our problems in things, nor in science and technology, nor in numbers of church members, nor in prestige, but in our close identification with Christ as our Living Lord.

The Methodist Men, the Woman's Society of Christian Service and the Wesleyan Service Guild, in addition to their service to the World Mission Program, reach out in service to the Penal Farm, to the Wesley House and Bethlehem Center, and to other areas of great need in the city.

At the February meeting of the Official Board, Ben Carpenter introduced a resolution which was wholeheartedly adopted by the Administrative Board:

That the Official Board of Christ Methodist Church is in full accord with the Memphis Police Department in its drive against pornography, salacious literature and immoral movies. This material can serve only to pollute the minds and morals of those who are exposed to it. That in order to keep Memphis a city clean in its morals and suited for raising families, the members of this Board will do all they can to oppose this type of material.

On another occasion, in September 1967, when the city was voting on the issue of "Liquor-By-The-Drink," the Official Board took action by passing a resolution:

> Resolved that the Official Board of Christ Methodist Church, Memphis, Tennessee, is Opposed To the Further Liberalization Of The Liquor Laws Of Tennessee And Is Therefore Opposed to "Liquor-By-The-Drink."

A quarter-page ad was placed in both the Memphis *Commercial Appeal* and the Memphis *Press Scimitar* stating the position of the Church and urging voters to vote against "Liquor-By-The-Drink."

In the days when the worship services were held in the Fellowship Hall, much of the time it was necessary to have two Sunday morning worship services. This was discontinued after we moved into the Sanctuary in 1964, but in two years' time there was discussion about the need for two Sunday morning services in the new Sanctuary. This spoke well for the ministry of Christ Church. In a called meeting of the Official Board, May 23, 1966, it was voted to initiate the 8:30 Sunday morning service for the months of June, July, August and September. The additional service then would be evaluated to determine whether to continue it thereafter.

The History Committee composed of Mrs. W. J. Templeton, Chairman, and Mrs. Fred M. Ridolphi and Mrs. P. B. Whitenton, presented their report of the work they had done in the period from June 1955 to the celebration of the Tenth Anniversary and into the beginning of 1966. They explained that this work had been a labor of love. Their only regret was that they were unable to list all the names of the persons who had been such dedicated volunteers as they builded the Church of Jesus Christ here on earth.

Christ Church had been considering the sponsoring of another new church when, in May 1966, the Executive Committee of the District Board of Church Extension selected a site for a new church facing Highway 70 and extending back to Munson Road. After deliberate consideration, a plan was worked out whereby Christ Church would be the sponsor, and it was also announced that Reverend Edward Horton was to be the minister of this new church to be named "Good Shepherd Methodist Church." This plan constituted a special tie between the two churches, since Reverend Horton was the first person to be licensed to preach from Christ Church. This sponsorship added another area of ministry and mission in our outreach to others in the city of Memphis.

It was announced that Dr. Grant had been appointed a delegate to the World Methodist Conference meeting in London, England in August 1966. Later Dr. and Mrs. Grant reported this World Conference experience as a treasured landmark for them.

The Lay Witness Mission Movement, under the direction of Dr. Ben Johnson, was proving a blessing to both individuals and churches. Dr. Tom Shipmon introduced Dr. Ben Johnson to speak to the Church Board and at the conclusion, they voted to sponsor a Lay Witness Mission in the Church, November 18, 19, 20, 1966. Good things continued to happen. At the October 1966 Official Board Meeting it was announced that Dr. Robert Goodrich and Bill Mann of First Methodist Church of Dallas, Texas would be in the city at Christ Church to conduct revival services, November 27-30, 1966. These services followed the Lay Witness Mission and made the month of November a spirit-filled month. These two great spiritual experiences made a profound impression on all whose lives were touched. In the Lay Witness Mission forty-two consecrated men and women from eight states came to live among us and share with us. From the moment of their arrival until the moment of farewells when they left for their homes, the hours were filled with spiritual enrichment. The leadership of Dr. Ben Johnson, the public mass meetings, the coffee groups in the homes, the small groups sharing at the church, and many personal contacts made us recognize our oneness in Christ. The spiritual lift became perpetuated by many small Sharing Groups within the congregation. All who attended and heard the superb team of Dr. Goodrich and Bill Mann as they preached and sang the Gospel were exhilarated and inspired beyond words, and only eternity can reveal how far-reaching these services may have been.

Another milestone was reached when John Studstill was secured as an additional missionary. It was announced that he would be serving in the Belgian Congo and that Christ Church had the distinction of being one of the top fifteen churches in the nation in missionary giving.

A report of the Methodist Men organization for Christ Church in 1966-67 revealed that only about half of the men who are members of the church are members of a Sunday School Class. One of the goals of the Methodist Men was to increase participation in the Sunday School Classes and to increase the enrollment of men in the Methodist Men's group. They continued to emphasize personal and spiritual growth through good programs and worthwhile projects. Some of their projects have been local missions and sponsorship of Scout Troops. Great emphasis was placed on participation and cooperation with the work of the Commission on Membership and Evangelism by setting up Prayer Groups preceding the Church's "Venture of Faith" program. Methodist Men have continued to devote great emphasis to the Retreat at Lake Junaluska, North Carolina, which is scheduled each year during the last weekend in July. Often the Memphis Conference has led in attendance at this important spiritual opportunity, and often Christ Church has led the Conference by having the largest number of men in attendance.

At the Charge Conference on May 1, 1967, the records show that these persons were recommended as Lay Speakers:

David Bencomo	Sam Mays
Sewell Dunkin	Marion Meadows
Ernest Felts	John Parsons
Bert Ferguson	Jack Renshaw
David Foster	John Rhodes
Jac Gates	Dr. Tom Shipmon
Roy Greenlee	Dr. W. J. Templeton
Tom Jamieson	Keith Weisinger
Burns Landess	Max Winn
Morris Liming	

The Annual Meeting for the Conference Woman's Society of Christian Service and the Wesleyan Service Guild met at Christ Methodist Church, Memphis, Tennessee, April 13-15, 1967. The women of the Church, under the leadership of Mrs. Oscar B. Crofford, had made elaborate preparations for this important meeting. The theme of this Annual Meeting was "In Thy Light We Walk." Mrs. James B. Green was Conference President.

The attendance and enrollment of the Sunday School increased under the leadership of Bill Crump, Director of Christian Education, and in addition to the regular Sunday School Classes (with some reorganization of departments), the Youth Fellowship, the Scouts, and the Athletic Program, all moved forward. One of the emphases in the field of Christian Education which was bearing fruit was the "New Day" program that was being stressed throughout the entire Church.

Along with a theme to encourage Christ Church to study and practice "Christianity in Depth," Reverend Charles Lynn, Minister of Evangelism, who had come in June 1967 to join the staff, insisted on enthusiastic participation in the 1967 Fall School of Religion. In this program there were fourteen courses scheduled to include the Children, Youth, and Adult Divisions of the Church. August 13, 1967 was set aside for "Prayer Commitment Sunday," with the staff thereby hoping that each member would make a definite commitment to prayer.

It was gratifying that two young men were requesting at the Charge Conference of 1967 licenses to preach. They were Keith Rice, a member of Christ Church who was a student in the Divinity School of Yale University in New Haven, Connecticut and William Lloyd Smith, Jr., son of Mr. and

Mrs. William Lloyd Smith, Sr., a student at the University of the South at Sewanee, Tennessee.

The year 1968 continued to bring showers of blessings in a vast number of ways. Dr. Ben Johnson came back for a Sunday engagement as Guest Minister; another Sunday was devoted to honoring our certified lay-speakers of the congregation; Dr. Kermit Long from the General Board of Evangelism led us in our revival services; and the January Bible Conference was led by Dr. Mack B. Stokes of Emory University. Beginning on Palm Sunday and continuing through Holy Week there were special services with Dr. Thomas A. Carruth of Asbury Theological Seminary leading in a Prayer Enrichment Seminar to be followed by services on Maundy Thursday with the celebration of Holy Communion and the rendition of "The Seven Last Words" by the Chancel Choir. On Good Friday there was an Ecumenical Service with Father Paul W. Clunan of St. Louis Catholic Church, Memphis, as the speaker.

The Pastor's Report to the Charge Conference on April 1, 1968 made reference to this Charge Conference as being the last one before the General Conference meeting in Dallas, Texas, which was scheduled to be the General Conference that would unite the then Methodist Church and the Evangelical United Brethren Church. A number of other Conferences and Committees have been meeting for the last several years with representatives from both Churches to work out plans for their merging that would be mutually acceptable to both groups. April 23, 1968 had been programmed as the day for the merger to occur during the session of the General Conference, held in Dallas. Dr. Grant stated that out of this merger would come some structural and legislative changes and perhaps some changes in terminology; however, the all-encompassing purpose and passion of the Church will remain the same: namely, to preach a vital personal message that only Christ can save the world and that he gave His life to seek and to save the lost.

An interesting church record to read is the called session of the Charge Conference, November 1967, to authorize the purchase of the Lee. C. Roundtree property at 382 East Cherry Circle. The purchase price was $70,000, with a down payment and three notes for the remainder, bearing six percent interest, to be paid at intervals as specified.

Another called session of the Church's Charge Conference, August 19, 1968, was for the purpose of accepting the resignation of Paul Schultz, who had been the Director of Music since 1965, and for presenting the recommendation of the Music Committee to hire Mr. and Mrs. Charles H. Noble, Jr. The Nobles had been Choir Director and Organist at First Methodist Church, Sebring, Florida. Details were executed, and they began their work on September 1, 1968 and lived in the "Roundtree Property" recently purchased by the Church. In a later church report Mr. Noble was listed as a Local Preacher and the report listed the following groups under his direction:

Chancel Choir, Men's Chorus, Men's Quartette, three Children's Choirs, a Youth Choir, an Interpretative Choir, a Girls' Ensemble, Solos, Duets, Trios of Instrumental Music, and Guest Musicians. Additionally, time was to be spent in home visitation and recruitment.

In November 1968, upon recommendation of Dr. Grant and by action of the Official Board, David Cauley was hired as the Director of Christian Education, to succeed Bill Crump who had resigned to take another position.

The Architect and Building Committee with Jack Renshaw, Chairman, continued to study the needs of the congregation for a Recreation-Classroom Complex. Ed Thorn, Architect, was requested to continue the study of proposed plans and provide sketches for a December 1968 meeting.

In a report given by Reverend Charles Lynn, an Interdenominational Youth Rally with a theme "Something Ridiculous," attracted 4,015 Youth for the six nights of the rally. Reverend Keith Tonkel of Gulfport, Mississippi, was the speaker for this Youth Rally. Fifty-two churches of eight denominations were represented. It was such a success that the youth immediately began plans for another similar rally entitled, "Something Else," to be held the next year. Bill Barnard was President of the Youth Department and he also represented the Youth of the Church on many occasions, especially in reporting to the members of the Official Board.

The fall 1968 evangelistic endeavor had the theme, "Action—Reaction." Dr. Ben Johnson of Atlanta led the program.

Genuine compassion and Christian concern were manifested in the support of Inner-City Missions under the direction of Mrs. Elizabeth Poole. This work relates largely to the United Methodist Neighborhood Centers and the Prospect Day Care Center, both located in Memphis. By the end of this calendar year of 1968, the Crisologos were in the United States again for a furlough and visit, and they visited us at Christmas. The entire Missionary Budget was $37,387.

In early 1969, Dr. Grant made the following announcement:

> Following months of earnest prayer concerning the tenure of our ministry in Christ Church we have decided it would be best for the Church and us for our ministry here to be terminated this June. I have apprised Bishop Finger, Dr. James Fisher [the District Superintendent] and our Pastoral Relations Committee of this decision.
>
> In the United Methodist Church one must retire at 72, or may retire at 65. I'll reach 65 before Annual Conference in June. Because of our deep love for Christ, our love for people, our pure enjoyment in preaching God's word and because of the excellent

health both Mary Anna and I have, we have asked Bishop Finger
for another assignment.

Following Dr. Grant's decision to ask for another appointment at the
1969 Annual Conference, on May 7th the congregation honored Dr. and
Mrs. Grant with an appreciation dinner. They were presented with a gift of
silver and a check and also some "gag gifts" to add fun to the evening. It was a
delightful evening and long to be remembered by everyone who had come
to pay tribute and to express their love and affection for a couple who had
served God so faithfully. Dr. Grant was the organizing Pastor and had been
the Senior Minister for the entire fourteen years of the life of the Church.
The congregation began with 600 Charter Members and had grown during
the fourteen years to 2,610 on April 1, 1969.

Following the action of the 1968 General Conference, which was the
uniting Conference for the merger of the Methodist Church with the Evangelical United Brethren Church, the official name of the Church was changed
in May 1969 to Christ United Methodist Church.

Mr. and Mrs. Charles Noble who had been our Minister of Music and
Organist since September 1968 notified the Official Board of their resignation to accept a position in Kentucky, effective July 1, 1969.

These were busy days for the women and others of Christ Church who
planned not only the appreciation dinner on May 7, 1969 for Dr. and Mrs.
Grant but also planned a reception for Mr. and Mrs. Noble and Reverend
and Mrs. Charles Lynn, who were leaving the staff for an appointment in
Benton, Kentucky. The reception was planned for Sunday evening, June 8,
1969, following the service when Reverend Lynn would preach his final
message before going to his new appointment. In addition to these events,
thoughts were also turning toward plans to welcome a new minister and his
family. Dr. Grant's message to the congregation was printed on the front of
the bulletin for June 8, 1969, his last Sunday:

> To the Members of Christ United Methodist Church: It has been
> my great joy to share in the dreams, decisions, the efforts and the
> rich fellowship of the past fourteen wonderful years as the Pastor
> of Christ United Methodist Church. My personal preference
> would be to remain forever in the fellowship of so great a church,
> and so wonderful a people. My professional judgement dictates
> otherwise.
>
> One reason the United Methodist Church has become one of
> the greatest on the face of the earth is its itinerant system — its
> practice of making fresh ministerial leadership available to local

churches in a smoothly operating manner.

Sunday—June 8—will be my last message, thus bringing to a close our formal Pastor-Parishioner relationship, but Christian friendship can and will continue. Mrs. Grant joins me in expressing our deep affection for you and our great appreciation for all that you have done and been.

Signed—Charles W. Grant

The Vision Lives On

... the voice of the Lord saying, Whom shall I send, and who will go for us? Then said I, Here am I; send me.

— *Isaiah 6:8 (KJV)*

The fifteenth year of Christ United Methodist Church began with the arrival of a new Senior Minister, Dr. J. Harold Beaty.

The Pastor-Parish Committee had spent many hours in meetings and in consultations with Bishop Finger and the District Superintendent, Dr. James A. Fisher, searching for just the right minister to fill the pulpit at Christ Church. Dr. Beaty came highly recommended. He was a native of Georgia and had been a distinguished leader and pastor in the South Georgia Conference, coming to Memphis from the First Methodist Church of Thomasville, Georgia. Prior to World War II, during which he served as an officer in the Marines, Dr. Beaty had earned a degree in law. At age thirty, he made the decision to enter the ministry and enrolled in Candler School of Theology at Emory University in Atlanta, where he earned both the Bachelor of Divinity and the Master of Divinity degrees. Later he enrolled at Florida State University and received his Doctor of Philosophy degree. With each degree, he graduated with high honors. He and Mrs. Beaty, Stella, were the parents of four children: Stella, Louise, Jim, and Cathy.

On June 18, 1970, the Church honored Dr. and Mrs. Beaty and Reverend and Mrs. Paul W. Clayton, the new Associate Minister and his wife, with a beautiful reception in the Fellowship Hall. The Claytons, Paul and his wife, Carolyn, with their two children, Wesley and Amy, had come to Memphis from Ridgely, Tennessee. Both parsonages were freshened up with paint and remodeling as well as with some new furnishings.

There was some discussion of selling the Parsonage at 4227 Belle Meade Cove and securing a lot that was available on the west side of Grove Park, about three lots north of the Church property line, and building a new parsonage for the Senior Minister. Later, this lot was secured for future use.

The Church responded well to the new Ministers, and Dr. Beaty expressed his delight with the number of people who were attending church, at a time when many were saying there was a drop-off in church attendance. Plans were made for a five month program for the Church, to be called "The Festival of Faith." This was designed for all the work areas and commissions to encourage a renewal of faith in every area of the life of the Church.

The Architect and Building Committee had under consideration for several years the need for more classrooms and an activities building. It was not long until their dream began to progress and become a reality. The Finance Committee under the Chairmanship of Harold Benson began the planning of the Stewardship Program to insure the needs of the Budget for 1970. It was directed by William A. Perry and it was called the "Joy of Giving." The pledges were for a twelve month period and would be used for both the Operating Budget and the Building Fund. The goals were reached and even were exceeded. Someone expressed it thus, "The 'Joy of Giving' program brought with it the joy of accomplishment and the joy of service."

The Music Committee and others had been in search of a Minister of Music. It was announced in November 1969, that Don Sanford and his wife, Marjorie would begin work with the choirs at Christ Church, February 1, 1970. Don Sanford was a native of Massachusetts and a graduate of Boston University with a major in sacred music. Mrs. Sanford, also an excellent musician, was a native of New Albany, Mississippi, with a degree in public school music. They planned an extensive Ministry of Music with a number of choirs.

In May 1970, a contract was signed with radio station KWAM to broadcast the Sunday morning worship services—this would further extend the ministry of Christ Church to all parts of the city. Later, a note was received from a listener on a jet plane at an altitude of 21,000 feet. His comment was, "I heard part of the service and it came in loud and clear. What a blessing I received."

Jesse Vineyard, Lay Leader for the Church, reported to the Bishop and District Superintendent, "The new Ministers, Dr. Beaty and Reverend Paul Clayton, have been well received and the Church is continuing to move forward."

One of the new programs in the Music Ministry was the use of Handbells. It was decided that these would be purchased with private donations. After being trained by Don Sanford, the group shared its music with the congregation on special occasions. Three new youth choirs had been started and

Dr. James Harold Beaty

Mrs. Stella C. Beaty

the number responding to the music ministry had been gratifying.

When Mrs. Elizabeth Poole who had been our worker in the Inner-City Ministry resigned, the Church hired Franklin Perry who had been trained by Mrs. Poole both at Bethlehem Center and the Neighborhood Center to continue this much needed ministry. He, who became the Inner-City Missionary, was a very skilled and well-qualified person with a number of years' experience.

As the end of the 1970 Conference year approached, Dr. Beaty stated in one of the church bulletins, "The true disciples are 'doers' and not 'hearers'; the world grows better because people wish that it should and take the right steps to make it better." The report to Annual Conference stated that during the year of 1970 an average of 1900 people had participated in Sunday activities. During the weekdays the children, youth and adult programs (Scouts, Woman's Society of Christian Service, Day School, Men's Club, etc.) had attracted the participation of many, many additional people. The Church had received 232 new members, thirty-four of whom were on profession of faith. The pledges had amounted to $453,440 which included the operating budget, the benevolences and the money for the building fund.

During the Commencement Celebration at Lambuth College for 1970, John Parsons, dedicated member of Christ Church, was awarded the Doctor of Law degree. Dr. Parsons had given outstanding leadership and support to Lambuth College. Following his death, the Varsity Gymnasium of the Athletic Center was named in his memory.

Following Annual Conference 1970, Reverend Edward W. Walton, Jr. joined the staff as the Minister of Education. He had attended Lambuth College and Memphis State University, receiving his degree in 1963. He received both a Bachelor of Divinity degree and a Masters degree in Christian Education from the Candler School of Theology at Emory University. His most recent appointment and service was Minister of Education at Trinity United Methodist Church in Memphis. He and his wife, Marilyn, have two children—Cathy and Phil. The Church welcomed to the staff Mrs. Jane Gamble as Organist. She was a graduate of Lambuth College with her degree in Music. Later, she received her Doctors degree. Appreciation was expressed to Chris Mays who served as interim Organist.

In November 1970, there was excitement within the congregation. Dr. Winfield Dunn was elected Governor of the State of Tennessee. The Church *Courier* carried this statement:

> We take great pride in the fact that a member of our Church has been elected to the high office of Governor of Tennessee. Dr. Winfield Dunn and his wife, Betty, are charter members of Christ Church. He is Vice-Chairman of the Administrative

Board, a member of the Chancel Choir, and a teacher in the Kings-wood Class. Our prayers and good wishes will be with the Dunns in their dedication to this new responsibility.

In keeping with the tradition of making Christmas at Christ Church a very special time with memorial and honor poinsettias decorating the altar and choir loft, Mrs. Warner Howe designed a beautiful wreath in memory of her mother. The Chrismon Tree was dedicated on December 13 and lighted on December 22, 1970. The Chancel Choir presented "For Unto Us a Child Is Born" by J. S. Bach. The year of 1970 was closed with a Watch Night Service and the celebration of Holy Communion.

Because of changing of dates for the closing of the Conference Year from May 31 to December 31, the "Every Member Canvass" was designed for the pledges to be made on a nineteen month basis. The total budget outlined and proposed was for $522,519 and would cover the period from June 1, 1971 to December 31, 1972. This was the largest budget ever proposed for Christ Church.

One of the highlights for the year's activities for the Methodist Men's Club was the annual Father-Son Banquet, always with an outstanding speaker and program. The Laymen's Conference at Lake Junaluska continued to hold the keen interest of the Methodist Men. The Memphis Conference Men supported by a representation from Christ Church continued to excel in attendance. Dr. Tom Shipmon was the featured speaker this year, 1971, using as his subject, "This is My Witness and Ministry."

Reverend Howard Rash announced that after forty-three years of service in the ministry, he was officially retiring at the 1971 Annual Conference. He and his wife, Mary Evelyn, have been a great blessing to the congregation as they have served these years. He planned to continue some responsibilities on a limited basis and to live at 4210 Grandview Avenue in Memphis. On Sunday, May 23, 1971, the members of Christ Church honored Reverend and Mrs. Rash with a reception in the Fellowship Hall, after Reverend Rash had preached at the morning worship service. The statement on the front of the *Courier*, is a tribute to them:

No words can adequately describe what Mary and Howard Rash have meant to so many people in the Memphis area. Since coming to Memphis in 1939, they have served seven appointments in Shelby County and will complete eight years of service at Christ Church in June, 1971. Their sincerity and dedication are unexcelled. We rejoice that they will continue to be a part of our staff and congregation and we covet for them good health and joy for many years to come.

As a part of Christ Church's 1984 celebration of two hundred years of Methodism in America, Reverend and Mrs. Howard W. Rash presented to the congregation an ancient Communion Flagon. This flagon bearing the inscription "CENTENNIAL M. E. Church" was created by Reed and Barton, Silversmiths of Taunton, Massachusetts in 1884 to celebrate the hundredth birthday of The Methodist Episcopal Church, organized at the Christmas Conference of 1784 at Lovely Lane Chapel in Baltimore, Maryland. The Rash's first full-time Pastoral Appointment, following Reverend Rash's graduation from Drew Theological Seminary and Ordination, was 1931-1933 at Seabright, New Jersey near the entrance to New York harbor. This Centennial Flagon was used regularly there on the Lord's Table for the serving of Holy Communion. During the 1960's the Seabright congregation merged with a neighboring congregation. Since there was no need for two Communion Services, the Seabright Centennial silver service was sold. Mrs. Rash's sister who lived in New Jersey purchased the flagon and presented it to Reverend and Mrs. Rash, who treasured it greatly. After restoration of the flagon by the silversmiths, additional engraving was added to record its history and it was presented to Christ Church, Memphis, Tennessee. This historic flagon now continues to serve "the people called Methodists" with the Communion Wine of which our Lord said, "This is My blood shed for you for the forgiveness of sin. Drink ye all of this in remembrance of Me."

Christ Church in 1971 was supporting four missionary families in various parts of the world: Dr. and Mrs. Crisologo in Sarawak, Borneo; Reverend and Mrs. Heyer in Sierra Leone, West Africa; Reverend and Mrs. Gravely in Brazil and Reverend Cecil Kirk, Inner-City Mission in Memphis. They visit us when on furlough, and provide great inspiration toward the missionary giving. Dr. Beaty received a letter recently from the Board of Missions announcing that of the fifteen Churches making the largest contributions to the Advance Special Program, Christ Church now ranks seventh. Presently, we are giving one third as much to others as we spend on local programs.

The Christmas Season was made more beautiful this year, 1971, with the Chancel Choir rendering the Christmas portion of Handel's Messiah. The choir was accompanied by members of the Memphis Symphony Orchestra.

The Church was stunned to learn of the untimely death of Reverend Charles Lynn, February 12, 1972. He had served as the Minister of Evangelism for Christ Church from 1967-1969. He and his wife, Shirley, had been at First United Methodist Church, Benton, Kentucky, since leaving Memphis. His death followed open-heart surgery.

During the summer, 1972, and under the direction of Don Sanford, the Youth Choir made a Concert Tour through East Tennessee and Georgia, for which they received congratulatory letters complimenting their performance.

Mrs. Ray Drenner, a Charter Member, who had served for thirteen years as the Church Hostess and Dietician, retired. Many expressions of appreciation came to her for her years of service and for the bringing of happiness to so many people.

On July 23, 1972, a Church Conference was called to present the plans for the proposed construction of the "Activities Building" to provide additional spaces for classes and a recreational program. Reverend Paul Clayton presided and Ben Carpenter was elected secretary. The Chairman called on Jack Renshaw, Chairman of the Architect and Building Committee, to explain the purpose of the meeting. He then made the following motion:

> BE IT RESOLVED, that the recommendations of the Architect and Building Committee for the construction of the proposed Activities Building be, and the same are herewith approved and that the preliminary plans, and estimates of cost as obtained pursuit to preliminary plans dated July 18, 1972, prepared by Thorn, Howe, Stratton, and Strong, Architects, for the construction of said Activities Building be, and the same are herewith approved; and that the Architect and Building Committee is herewith authorized to take all necessary and proper action for the construction of said building. The Architect and Building Committee shall consist of Jack Renshaw, chairman, Kenneth Markwell, vice chairman, Ralph McCool, Lee B. McCormick, George T. Roberts, Sr., E. R. Richmond, Sr., Andrew A. Sippel, Jr., and Gene C. Williams.

> BE IT FURTHER RESOLVED, that the funds for the construction of said building be obtained from the Building Fund of Christ United Methodist Church and that a sum not to exceed $250,000 from said Building Fund be, and the same is herewith authorized for construction of said building and all work incidental thereto, including site preparation, furnishings and equipment in connection therewith.

> BE IT FURTHER RESOLVED, that authority is granted to Jack Renshaw, chairman of the Architect and Building Committee, D. A. Noel, chairman of the Administrative Board, Lee B. McCormick, president of the Board of Trustees and John Whitsitt, chairman of the Committee on Finance, to sign all contracts and any other papers necessary thereto on behalf of Christ United Methodist Church which may be required for the construction of said facilities. The signature of any two (2) of the above named shall be required on said contracts and papers.

The above motion was seconded by James H. Seabrook, Sr.

Later at another Church Conference in October 1972, the amount of money referred to in the above second Resolution was changed from $250,000 to $280,000. Thus, the wheels were set in motion by the action of the Church Conference on July 23, 1972 to begin work on the fourth building of the long-range plans.

During the year of 1972, the emphasis was on deepening and enriching our prayer lives. Dr. Charles Allen, Minister of First United Methodist Church of Houston, Texas, led us in meaningful days in which he emphasized Christian living and prayer. "You'll be happier if you live this way," he preached.

As plans were being made for the 1973 Budget, the goal for the operating fund was set at $350,000 along with a thirty-six month Building Fund Goal of $450,000. Dr. Floyd Hinshaw, a Methodist Minister under special assignment with the Board of Missions, came to direct us in our stewardship program. The members continued their good record of stewardship by subscribing the full amount. The theme for the year 1973 in the United Methodist Church was "KEY '73," with emphasis on six specific topics: Repentance and Prayer, The Word of God, The Resurrection, New Life, Proclamation, and Commitment. The second retreat for the Administrative Board and the staff of Christ Church was held at Pickwick Inn with the renowned English Minister, Canon Bryan Greene as the leader and speaker.

Following the Annual Meeting of the Women's Society of Christian Service and the Wesleyan Service Guild at St. John's Methodist Church in the Fall of 1972, it was announced that beginning in 1973 the women of the Memphis Conference would move into the new organization for women to be known as United Methodist Women. This was one of the changes in structure and nomenclature following the merger with the Evangelical United Brethren Church. Mrs. S. W. Grise was the last President of the former organization, named Woman's Society of Christian Service, and Mrs. Jesse Anderson was the first President of United Methodist Women at Christ Church. The organization for the women had more than 400 members enrolled, even though the congregation was less than twenty years old. It seems almost incredible that in so short a time the unit of United Methodist Women with fifteen circles had grown to be the largest in the Memphis Conference and also perhaps in the State of Tennessee.

June 10, 1973 is remembered as a very special time when Dale Brady came to be our first full-time Director of Recreation. Dale and his wife, Sandra, were the parents of a son named Braxton. The congregation was excited that we would have an activities program to meet the needs of all ages in fellowship and activities. We would also be seeking to make the best use of the new Activities Building. The date for the dedication of this building was scheduled for March 3, 1974, when Bishop Finger would be present to preach and lead in the Dedication Ceremony.

The New Year 1974, brought with it a number of changes: Mrs. Glenn Ragland, who had served as Membership Secretary for more than ten years was retiring and also Mrs. Avis D. Allen, who joined the church staff in 1959 as Financial Secretary, was finishing fifteen years of service. Receptions and appropriate recognition were given to both of them.

In getting the Activities Program started, Christ Church sponsored the first Christian Arts and Crafts Festival. This included Performing Arts, Visual Arts, Crafts and Literature.

In 1974, the nineteenth year of Christ Church began under the leadership of Dr. Beaty as the staff and Administrative Board went again to Pickwick Landing Inn for the Annual Retreat. Dr. James Buskirk, Professor of Evangelism at Candler School of Theology at Emory University, was the speaker and leader. The statistical report showed that at the conclusion of last year, 1973, the Church had 2800 members and 1454 persons in Sunday School. The financial report stated that during 1973, $689,270 was contributed by members of the Church. Wednesday night Fellowship dinners, with the fellowship, study, and a time of spiritual renewal, came to mean so much to so many. Now that the Activities Building was opened, the programs being offered by the Director, Dale Brady, for children, youth and others, brought added blessings.

During Holy Week, 1974, Dr. Beaty and Reverend Clayton brought messages from the theme, "Faces Around the Cross." The Choir, assisted by members of the Memphis Symphony Orchestra, presented on Palm Sunday the cantata, "The Holy City."

A reception was given for Mrs. Charles McVean, who was retiring as Director of the Christ Methodist Day School, after guiding its growth and development for fifteen years. She and her family were charter members of Christ Church and she had not only been a wonderful Christian, but also had been an effective teacher and administrator. As she retired, she was succeeded by Sam Drash.

Change is ever present with us, but it is a part of our growth and development. At Annual Conference, 1974, Reverend Paul Clayton was assigned to be the Pastor of Forest Heights United Methodist Church in Jackson, Tennessee. We regretted losing them, for he and Carolyn and their children, Wesley and Amy, had endeared themselves to many friends. They requested no reception be given, but a gift was presented and appreciation and best wishes were extended to them at the conclusion of the morning worship.

The beauty of the Methodist system is that when we lose one beloved minister, we are soon able to welcome another, so it was our good fortune to have as the new Associate Minister, Reverend Albert M. Evans. An informal reception was planned to welcome him and his wife, Betty, and daughters, Carla and Kathryn. Reverend Evans graduated from Southwestern in Memphis (now Rhodes College) and received his Seminary degree from the Vanderbilt Divinity School in Nashville, Tennessee. He had served as the Minister at Asbury United Methodist Church in Memphis and as the Associate Minister at St. Luke's United Methodist Church in Memphis. He had just completed three years as the Minister of Humboldt United Methodist Church, Humboldt, Tennessee.

October 6, 1974 was a very special Laity Sunday, in that Governor Winfield Dunn returned to Christ Church and gave the "Laity Day Address."

Following the death of Reverend Charles Lynn, Shirley Lynn returned to Memphis in 1972, and became a part of the Christ Church Staff. She has been a Church Visitor, a Secretary, an Assistant to the Ministers, and in 1975 she piloted a new program with "Singles Ministry." This program included persons never married and those who are single because of death or divorce.

The years, filled with so many wonderful and worthwhile blessings, pass quickly. It seems that not long after we have welcomed a New Year, we move rapidly through the services and programs and before we realize it, the Advent season is with us. With wonderful Christmas music and special worship services we celebrate once more the "Good News" of Jesus' birth.

A New Decade Begins

I must work the works of Him that sent me, while it is day...
—John 9:4 (KJV)

With the beginning of the New Year in 1975, Christ United Methodist Church was off to a fine start in celebrating our twentieth year of history. The year began with the Annual Retreat led by Dr. Elton Trueblood. He was the distinguished president of Yokefellows International, and a Professor at Earlham College, Richmond, Indiana. He is the author of many books, including *The Company of the Committed, A Place to Stand, The Incendiary Fellowship*. Dr. Trueblood was the Guest Minister in the Christ Church pulpit, January 26, 1975.

A new emphasis on Christian fellowship was being offered through the newly organized Single Adult Fellowship, the Keenager Group and the Fellowship Dinners.

The report of the Music Ministry given by Don Sanford stated that there were 207 participants. The new Kindergarten Choir had fourteen children enrolled. The New Covenant Singers scheduled their itinerary for their summer tour. The Plum Pudding Festival had become a tradition following the Christmas Musical Program.

The Church was blessed with the visit of Bishop Earl G. Hunt, Jr. of Charlotte, North Carolina who preached on Palm Sunday and throughout Holy Week.

The formal celebration of the Twentieth Anniversary was observed on June 1, 1975, with Dr. Charles W. Grant, the founding minister, preaching on the subject, "Adventure in Faith." During this time there was also an excellent presentation entitled, "Christ Church, Past, Present and Future." A brief *History of Christ Church* and a list of Ministers who had been with the Church from 1955 to 1975 were printed in the Church *Courier*.

Our missionaries, Dr. and Mrs. Crisologo, were home on furlough and came to visit during the Thanksgiving Season. They were being transferred from their assignment in Sarawak, Borneo to the Ba Hospital in the Fiji Islands.

It was during this year that the Administrative Board approved the sponsoring of a refugee family. At the beginning of the Christmas Season we received the announcement that a Cambodian family, the Chey Suon family, would be coming to us from Fort Chaffee, Arkansas. A committee composed of members of the Church in cooperation with United Methodist Women welcomed them and assisted them in getting settled: finding a place for them to live, helping them to adjust in language study and school, seeking employment with their receiving job training, and providing food and clothes as needed. This was indeed a new type of ministry and after physical and economic needs were met, the Church continued to give them spiritual support.

The Shepherd Program was a new service being developed throughout Methodism. Under the leadership of Dr. Frank Philpot, Board Members were asked to be Shepherds. Each Shepherd was to be responsible for eight or ten families, to keep in touch with them and alert them to special events and programs that would be available to them through the Church. There were approximately 148 groups within the membership of the Church.

As we approached the 1976 Bicentennial Celebration for our Nation, Sam Drash, Director of the Christ Methodist Day School, requested that the family of each child offer a special prayer in the Chapel Service each Friday. A Prayer Pillow was prepared, with each family designing a patch emphasizing some part of our Nation's history. This pillow was to be a gift for President and Mrs. Gerald Ford. Through special arrangements, the children were able to present the pillow to President Ford when he visited Memphis in May of 1976.

The Fifth Annual Retreat was held early in 1976 at the Holiday Inn University at Olive Branch, Mississippi. Dr. Arnold Prater, an outstanding speaker, writer, leader and Methodist Minister from Joplin, Missouri, was the leader.

Appreciation was expressed through words of Ralph McCool, Chairman of the Trustees, in the *Courier* of February 8, 1976, for the generous gift of the Sanctuary Organ by Mr. and Mrs. Jack Renshaw. We were eternally grateful to the Renshaws for this generous gift to Christ Church.

We were blessed during the winter season with the After Dinner Players from Houston, Texas. Their director and producer was Jeanette Clift George who played the role of Corrie Ten Boom in the film, *The Hiding Place*. When

A delegation of students from Christ Methodist Day School presented a "Whisper a Prayer" pillow to President Gerald Ford during his visit to Memphis in May 1976. Left to right: President Ford, Camille Harrison, Mike Drash, Doug Sparkman, Susan Burghen, Cliff Mitchell and an unidentified child. The pillow can now be seen in the Ford Library in Grand Rapids, Michigan.

Mrs. George spoke in the afternoon of February 19, 1976 in the Sanctuary, the house was filled to overflowing with people attending from every corner of the city as well as from the Mid-South.

In February, it was announced that Dr. Wayne A. Lamb, recently retired, had been employed as Minister of Evangelism of Christ Church. Dr. Lamb will work in a part-time capacity in the Area of Visitation. Dr. Lamb has served "with distinction, a number of important pulpits in the Memphis Conference," and he retired as District Superintendent of the Memphis-Asbury District at the recent Memphis Annual Conference. He and his wife, Dr. Susan Ruby Lamb, were currently a part of our congregation, and he was welcomed warmly to the Church staff.

In an expression of appreciation for her many years of service, a Ginkgo tree was planted in honor of Mrs. A. A. Sippel. Mrs. Sippel had served in an administrative capacity with the pre-school program of the Church.

Dr. Beaty was elected a Clerical Delegate to the United Methodist Church General Conference which met this time in Portland, Oregon.

Mrs. Ray Conder (Jan) was welcomed to the staff in May 1976, as Membership Secretary. Mrs. Gordon Steger who had been serving in the capacity was moving to Dallas. It became known also that Reverend Eddie Walton would be leaving at Annual Conference, 1976, to join the Conference Staff in Jackson, Tennessee. Following Annual Conference, June 1976, we welcomed to the staff the Reverend Robert H. Wood and Reverend Catherine L. Wood, a husband and wife clergy team. Bob and Cathy graduated from the Methodist Theological School of Ohio. They had each earned a Master of Divinity degree and a Master of Arts in Christian Education.

The boys and girls of the Day School were excited when they received a letter of appreciation from President Ford, thanking them and their teacher, Mrs. Dorris Smith, for the Prayer Pillow. Copies of the letter were made and each child was given a copy to take home. Quoted is part of the letter:

> It was a special pleasure to meet you during my visit to Memphis, and I want to thank you once again for the 'Whisper a Prayer' pillow. I deeply appreciate the time and effort that you and your families devoted to handcrafting this splendid Bicentennial gift. To know that you remember our Nation in your prayers is indeed heartening. I hope that your concern for our country's welfare will continue throughout your lives. With warm wishes to you and your teacher, Mrs. Carlos Smith.
>
> Signed: Sincerely, Gerald R. Ford

Following the Jurisdictional Conference, meeting at Lake Junaluska, announcement was made that our new Bishop would be Bishop Earl G.

Hunt, one of Methodism's great preachers and administrators.

Our fall week of Revival and Renewal, 1976, was led by Dr. and Mrs. Lawrence Lacour, from the First United Methodist Church of Colorado Springs, Colorado. He was a former Navy Chaplain and spent time in evangelistic work in Japan. Mildred Lacour was a professional harpist. She spoke to the women of the Church each morning from the subject, "The Modern Woman."

Our operating budget for 1977 was estimated at $475,000. William C. Smith was the Chairman of Stewardship, and it was announced in the *Courier* that by November 21 the pledges for the New Year had already exceeded the proposed budget.

Christmas this year, 1976, was made especially meaningful by the prepared Advent Banners—depicting The Trinity, The Glory of God, The Light of the World and Emmanuel. The Church was indebted to Mrs. Austin Trousdale and her mother, Mrs. Forrest Dowling, Jr., for these remarkable works of art.

The New Year 1977, was off to a good start with the Annual Retreat being held at Holiday City University, Olive Branch, Mississippi. The leader and speaker was Dr. James T. Laney of the Candler School of Theology at Emory University, who later became the President of Emory University.

The Guest Minister for the Holy Week services was Bishop Frank L. Robertson of Louisville, Kentucky. Special music was provided by our Organist, Jane Gamble and by the soloist of the Choir. The climax on Easter Sunday was Dr. Beaty's sermon entitled, "The Resurrection Story."

Christ Church cooperated fully with the city-wide Billy Graham Crusade, held in the Liberty Bowl Stadium during the month of May 1977. Dr. Tom Shipmon was the Congregational Chairman from Christ Church. There was full participation with leadership in Choirs and Counseling as well as with providing transportation and making liberal financial contributions.

The women, under the leadership of an Organizational Committee, began the work of making Needlepoint Kneeling Cushions for the Chancel and Predella areas in the Sanctuary; this project was possible because of a generous gift for this purpose. Mrs. Perry Cockerham (Indie) was commissioned to design the Kneeling Cushions. For more than two years, fifty-seven women of Christ United Methodist Church spent approximately 39,000 hours of time in this gift of service. It was calculated that 6,379,408 stitches were put into the needlepoint. It was calculated that it would have taken one person, working eight hours a day, five days a week, fourteen years to have completed this task. If they had been paid $5.00 per hour, the cost of the project would have been $205,000. The members of the Organizational Committee were Mrs. George Atkinson, Mrs. Howard Boone, Mrs. Thomas R. Dyer, Reverend Albert Evans, Mrs. Don Howdeshell and Mrs. J. E. Ruffin. On Sunday, May 28, 1978, these beautiful and impressive Kneeling Cushions were dedicated. The colors in the cushions were coordinated with the colors of the beautiful stained-glass windows in the Sanctuary, and together they add to the worshipful atmosphere. Brochures have been prepared and are available with the explanation of the symbolism that is displayed in the designs of the cushions; also listed are the women who made this gift possible.

In June 1978, following Annual Conference, Reverend Jerry Corlew joined the Christ Church Staff as Executive Minister. He has been Executive Director of the United Neighborhood Centers and was one of the persons involved in the development of Wesley Highland Towers, a 396 apartment project for the elderly. He also served for a time as Chaplain in the U. S. Army. He and his wife, Martha Ann, have two children, Steve and Anne.

Two of the goals set forth at Annual Conference were to increase the membership total by 12,000 during the year and to develop ministries for "Single Persons," which included single persons of all ages and single family units with single parents.

We were honored on Laity Sunday with a visit from R. H. (Red) Bond, of Dyersburg, Tennessee as the speaker. He is one of the outstanding laymen of Methodism and has served on the General Board of Discipleship.

In considering the financial needs of the Church for 1979, $94,000 was placed in the budget for purchasing the lot at East Cherry and Poplar Avenue. Later, this property indeed was purchased.

The Lenten Season was made more significant this year as we shared in the World Hunger Project, which included Bangladesh, Korea, Sri Lanka, and Honduras. Bishop William R. Cannon preached during the Holy Week and the Choir presented again for our inspiration Dubois' "Seven Last Words."

Sunday, May 6, 1979, was a long awaited occasion. It was the Dedication of Christ Church buildings to the glory and service of God. Bishop Earl G. Hunt led us in the grand service of worship and dedication. It was a thrill to know that in fifteen years the $1,000,000 mortgage on the Sanctuary and Education Building had been paid. This high moment with the burning of the note was followed by dinner for the congregation in the Courtyard.

The Reverend Robert and Reverend Catherine Wood, the Associate Ministers who had been in charge of the Youth and Education Work of the Church, were assigned to another appointment. Reverend Pamela K. McDaniel, whose home had been in Mayfield, Kentucky, came to join the staff. She was a graduate of Duke University, Durham, North Carolina.

June 17, 1979, the first Sunday following Annual Conference, was recognized as the Tenth Anniversary of Dr. Beaty's ministry with us as Senior Minister. Gratitude was expressed for his faithful and outstanding leadership during these years. Four Diaconal Ministers in our congregation were recognized, two of whom were on the staff: Don Sanford, Minister of Music and Shirley Lynn, Administrative Assistant. The others were Mary Louise

Caldwell and Clarence Hampton, certified in Christian Education. (Diaconal Ministers are lay persons consecrated for special service in the Church.) Some of the special emphases for this year were: Small group ministry (such as the Men's Intercessory Prayer Group which has been in ministry for more than twenty years), Family Bible School, a course on our Wesleyan Heritage presented by Dr. W. E. Knickerbocker, the Trinity Bible Series (disciplined Bible Study) taught by Reverend Jerry Corlew, and a "Come as you are Bible Study" taught by Shirley Lynn and Dr. Beaty. Melinda Rauscher was welcomed to the staff on a part-time basis as Director of Children's Work.

A special Sunday was designated to stress the work and the needs of the Reelfoot Rural Ministry; the response was overwhelming. Later in the year at Christmas, the gifts of food wrapped in white were given to the Neighborhood Centers.

The New Year 1980 dawned with hope and expectancy—this would be the year celebrating the Twenty-fifth Anniversary of the founding of Christ United Methodist Church. Dr. Beaty preached the first sermon of the New Year, which he entitled "A Fresh Start." This was the year that the church-wide Evangelical Program was based on the theme "Proclaim the Word." The guest speaker to initiate this program was Dr. Jeff Fryer of Nashville, Tennessee. Television Ministry had been considered for some time as another important way to relate to people, so this was the year that Christ Church began broadcasting the Sunday morning worship service over Channel 3, WREG Television.

March 1980 was the beginning of a new ministry, "The Positive Christian Singles." This plan included all age groups, and Shirley Lynn was the teacher of the Sunday School Class where the emphasis was on spiritual growth and fellowship. The program was for those who have never married, and for those who are single through divorce or widowed by death. For Fellowship, the groups are the Young and Single (18-35), the Social Singles (30-55), and the Super Singles (55+). The activities of these groups include Bible Study, Social Service, Visiting the Nursing Homes, and Fellowship; for example, dinners, plays, movies, symphonies, pizza and putt-putt parties, retreats and a host of other events.

Dr. Charles Swindoll, enthusiastic minister, author, national television and radio speaker and pastor of the First Evangelical Free Church of Fullerton, California, was a guest speaker at Christ Church during March, 1980.

The Twenty-fifth Anniversary Celebration for Christ Church was observed on June 15, 1980. The goals for this day were 1000 in Sunday School, 1500 at the Morning Worship and 1000 at the Celebration Picnic.

United Methodist Women recognized and participated further in an outreach program in which they previously had been involved, Reading Is Fundamental (R.I.F.), with the children of LaRose School. The money given by groups was matched by government funds to buy good reading books for under-privileged children. The women had been a part of this program for seven years.

One of the Circles of United Methodist Women made Needlepoint Badges for the Christ Church Ushers. These were dedicated in honor of Mr. Charles McVean, who was one of the first ushers twenty-five years ago.

A happy occasion was the Fiftieth Wedding Anniversary of Reverend Howard and Mary Evelyn Rash, which was celebrated with a beautiful reception given by their children and grandchildren.

On September 10, "The Miracles," a choral group from the Baddour Memorial Center of Senatobia, Mississippi, an agency of the North Mississippi Methodist Conference, visited us and presented an outstanding musical program. This Center was established as a ministry and a home for handicapped persons. "The Miracles" have become quite famous as ambassadors from the Center and from the ministry there.

Following the Jurisdictional Conference which met in July 1980 at Lake Junaluska, the Memphis Conference welcomed a new bishop, Bishop Edward L. Tullis, who had served for eight years in the South Carolina area. A year later, in 1981, he was our Guest Minister for the Holy Week services.

We began the New Year 1981 by welcoming to the staff Marvin Budd, who had come from the First Methodist Church in Kingsport, Tennessee. Being a Diaconal Minister, his major responsibility was to be in Education, programming and working with the Council on Ministries. His wife, Tempe, is a native Memphian.

One of the enjoyable features for everyone was the visit and ministry through music of the University of Tennessee Chattanooga Singers under the direction of Dr. Glenn Draper. They are perhaps better known to us as the "Junaluska Singers" under his direction. This group has become world-famous as they have sung in many parts of the United States as well as in Russia and Europe.

Following a Program on Prayer developed and outlined by Dr. Thomas Carruth, the Church entered into a covenant of praying each day for our President, our nation, the world and ourselves.

The Easter Season 1981 was climaxed with the largest attendance in the history of Christ Church. A total of 2485 persons attended the morning worship services on Easter Sunday. Dr. Beaty challenged the people through the leadership of the Administrative Board in six areas:

1. Deepen the spiritual life of the membership of Christ Church.
2. Apply Christian principles to the life of the community.
3. Continue and increase our support of the Missional priorities of the Church at home and abroad.

4. Encourage each member to become an evangelist, speaking a good word for Jesus each day.
5. Complete the Maintenance Endowment Fund, continue work on wills and legacies.
6. Pray daily for each other, our Missionaries, persons in need, and the entire program of the Church.

Thirty-four persons who were members of our congregation had died during the past eighteen months. On Memorial Sunday, 1981, a special Bulletin was printed with all thirty-four names and a paragraph of biographical information about each person. Dr. Beaty used as his sermon topic, "Lest We Forget." Three ideas were stressed:

First, when we cross over to the other side, our Lord himself will be there to receive us. Second, the Scripture teaches that eternal life begins on earth and continues in Heaven. We think of death as a going away, Jesus thought of it as a coming home, a celebration, a time of rejoicing, a continuation of life that began on earth. Third, the Bible teaches another immortal truth: Every human soul is precious to God.

He quoted from Helen Emmons' book *In Search of a Crown:*

When my son died in early manhood, I knew then if I were ever to believe in life after death, I would have to believe it now. God would never waste a young life such as his with its promise of leadership and service to the world. Such a life must find its fulfillment—if not here, then in another life.

The Administrative Board was called in special session to hear the report of the Feasibility Committee. In the absence of the Chairman, Keith Weisinger, Gene Williams presented the report. It consisted of the adoption of a Master Plan, which called for a 10,000,000 square foot expansion to the Activities Building by adding classrooms to three sides of the present gymnasium, the construction of a utility building and "on premises parking" that would provide spaces for 180 cars in three parking lots. The projected cost was $656,000 and it was recommended that work begin when $200,000 in funds had been received. The remaining cost was to be amortized over a three-year period. Both the Administrative Board and the Congregation voted to accept this plan.

Progress and growth were reflected in the large Confirmation Class of forty-three boys and girls received into the membership of the Church on

May 31, 1981. Dr. Lamb reported that Christ Church Membership had reached 3500. It is a thrill and a joy to know that the Church continues to grow.

Seldom does a congregation experience such pain and sadness as occurred on November 6, 1981. The Memphis *Commercial Appeal* of November 8, 1981 carried the story of the tragic deaths of our beloved minister, Dr. J. Harold Beaty, and Mrs. Stella C. Beaty. The report of the Shelby County Medical Examiner's Office stated that Mrs. Beaty shot her former husband, Dr. J. Harold Beaty, and then killed herself. The congregation as well as the city was stunned and in deep sorrow, so the Sunday morning worship service, November 8, was a special Prayer Service led by Reverend Jerry Corlew and Mrs. Shirley Lynn. A joint funeral service was held at Christ Church on November 9, 1981. Bishop Edward L. Tullis and Bishop Earl G. Hunt brought messages at the Service.

The sermon that Dr. Beaty had prepared to preach on November 8 was entitled: "Up To Jerusalem." It is based on Mark 10:32, where Jesus is leaving the quiet hills, the villages and people of Capernaum and going up to Jerusalem where dangers and death await Him. In the closing paragraph, it is almost as if he sensed the danger ahead:

> God turns tragedy into beauty when we place ourselves and our circumstances in his keeping. Jesus demonstrated this when he left Galilee, went into Jerusalem, faced his destiny head-on. In similar manner you and I must face ours.

The *Courier* for November 15th, 1981, carried a beautiful tribute to Dr. Beaty:

TRIBUTE

> Someone has written, "The facts of life and death are neutral. It is our *response* that gives suffering a positive or negative meaning." WE can respond to the tragic death of Harold Beaty: "I knew it! Life's not fair. God doesn't care." Or we can respond: "I knew it! Life's not fair. But God is good."
>
> God is good because he let us have some time with His great servant. No man was more humble, more truly on the inside what he appeared to be on the outside. And it might have been we could have lived and died and never heard his laugh, his sermons. We might never have seen his smile, the light of his tremendous faith. We might have missed seeing how a spiritual giant handles earthly troubles.
>
> We can respond: "Life is unfair, but God is good because even

now he is bringing out good in grief." We are seeing the spirit of
God in ourselves. Why are we so outraged at senseless death?
Rabbi Harold Sikushner has suggested our hatred of everything
harmful is a result of God's spirit in our hearts. We are legiti-
mately angry at illness, angry that some illnesses still result in
death in spite of physicians' best efforts. Like God we love all His
children, hate anything hurtful to them. We see it is the spirit of
God in us that causes us to cling together now, loving, helping
each other. OUR response to tragedy can be: God is good because
He is teaching that He needs each of us. A great light had gone
out. We are privileged to trim our own lamp and make up part of
the loss. When Dr. Beaty went out of town, he always told the
office staff where he could be reached. Going out the door,
he would turn, lift a hand and say, "Now, you know where I
am." Having gone out the door of earthly life on wings of his
faith and our love, we *know* where he is. God grant we may follow
in his train.

In the last report made by Dr. Beaty for the Charge Conference, he spoke
of the influx of young families into the Church, making it necessary to re-
arrange many of the Church School Classes. At that time, there were sixty-
four infants on the preparatory rolls in the Cribs and Toddlers section of the
Nursery and forty-five two-year-olds in that section of the Nursery. Also
reported was a new ministry to the Singles of our congregation and community. Under the dynamic leadership of Shirley Lynn, a singles group called
"Positive Christian Singles" was organized. From the very beginning, this
ministry has revitalized a most important segment of the membership;
in fact, it has become a model for other churches to use as they develop a
similar ministry. From the very beginning, this group has had more than
one hundred members on roll and is ministering to perhaps three times
that number. Dr. Beaty also stated that Evangelism continued to be a top
priority and he commended the superb work in Visitation Evangelism being
done by Dr. Wayne Lamb. "The number of calls he makes each month is
incredible. Statistics, as impressive as they are, cannot begin to describe the
impact of this important ministry." The assimilation program of the new
members is unmatched anywhere. Each new member is assigned a sponsor,
invited to meet with the Senior and Executive Minister, invited to a "New
Member Party," and asked to attend an orientation class to study Methodist
doctrine, history, and polity.

Bishop Tullis, in consultation with the District Superintendent, Reverend
Joe Shelton, announced the appointment of Reverend Jerry Corlew, the
Executive Minister, as the Interim Pastor for the Church, while the Pastor-

Parish Committee began their work of securing a new Senior Minister for Christ Church.

During this period, Dr. Jane Gamble, who had served well as Organist, resigned to enter other employment and Mrs. Emily J. McAllister became the new Organist March 1, 1982.

It is always a high moment in the life of a congregation when one of the members feels the call of God to go into full time Christian service. At the Charge Conference in December, 1981, Myra Bennett Antwine was recommended as a candidate for the ordained ministry. She is the daughter of Mr. and Mrs. Milton Bennett. Mrs. Bennett (Gynette) was employed at the church office in 1966, then later was Dr. Charles Grant's secretary; she became Financial Secretary following the retirement of Mrs. Avis Allen in 1974. Mr. Bennett is Superintendent of church maintenance.

By popular request, a volume of Dr. Beaty's sermons was published and made available to members of the congregation and friends. Shirley Lynn, as editor, spent many hours preparing the material for this cherished volume.

At a called meeting of the Administrative Board, it was recommended and passed unanimously to name the Activities Building in memory of Dr. Beaty.

For Such a Time as This

*And who knoweth whether thou art come to the kingdom for such a
time as this?*
—Esther 4:14 (KJV)

Come Holy Spirit, Heavenly Dove
With all Thy quickening powers,
Come shed abroad a Saviour's Love
And that will quicken ours.
—from a hymn by Isaac Watts

Early in 1982, Bishop Edward L. Tullis announced the appointment of a
new Senior Minister for Christ Church. The *Commercial Appeal* carried a
feature story entitled, "Church's New Minister Is Preacher And Editor." The
newspaper story explained:

> Dr. Maxie D. Dunnam, newly appointed Senior Minister of Christ
> United Methodist Church in Memphis, is described by Bishop
> Tullis as 'one of the world's outstanding Methodist leaders.' He
> will visit the Church and preach at the morning worship on
> February 7, and then assume the position of Senior Minister,
> March 28. Presently he is serving as World Editor of *The Upper
> Room*, which Bishop Tullis says is the most widely distributed
> devotional guide in the world. He has been in this office in Nash-
> ville for almost ten years.

Dr. Dunnam is quoted as saying: "I am filled with anxiety along with the excitement of coming to Memphis. Anxiety because I'm leaving what has been the most fulfilling aspect of my life ministry; excitement because this is what I really am, a local Pastor—a Minister."

While in Nashville, Dr. Dunnam led the Methodist Church Prayer Fellowship Movement and at the same time achieved fame as an author and editor. In addition to his years as Editor of *The Upper Room*, he has written a number of books including *Dancing at My Funeral*, a personal testimony of his spiritual experience; *Barefoot Days of the Soul*, which deals with the subject of eternal life; several workbooks on prayer, to be used in small group study; *Alive in Christ;* and *Jesus Claims and Our Promises. The Workbook of Living Prayer* has been translated into the Spanish language, the Mandarin Chinese language, and it has been requested that it be translated into the Japanese language. Dr. Dunnam also wrote *The Communicator's Commentary: Galatians, Ephesians, Philippians, Colossians, and Philemon*, which is Volume VIII in a fifteen volume set, with Lloyd Ogilvie as Series Editor. *Our Journey: A Wesleyan View of the Christian Way* by Dr. Dunnam is a deft explication of "that which is the heartbeat, the distinct content, and to some degree the style of who we are as United Methodists—particularly as viewed by John Wesley" (Introduction, viii). The booklet of daily devotions for Lent, *The Sanctuary*, has been written by Dr. Dunnam for six years, beginning in 1980. In Emmitsburg, Maryland in January 1986, the meeting of the Ecumenical Institute of Spirituality, which Dr. Dunnam will chair, will be held. Additionally, he is a member of the Board of Directors for the Academy of Spiritual Formation at the Upper Room, Nashville, Tennessee, and Program Chairman for the World Methodist Council which meets every five years. This world gathering of Methodists in July 1986 will be in Nairobi, Kenya, East Africa and will be televised to the world by satellite. Dr. Dunnam has worked for at least two years making ready the program for these proceedings. Yet with all these experiences, Dr. Dunnam readily confessed that his first love is the pulpit; in fact, he had said to Bishop Tullis earlier that he would like to return to the pastorate. Bishop Tullis speaks of this as a purposeful appointment. "We're bringing a strong evangelical leader to Memphis and we're bringing one of the world's outstanding Methodist leaders to Memphis."

In 1982, Christ United Methodist Church was the largest United Methodist congregation in the State of Tennessee, with approximately 3,500 members. At the time of the arrival of Dr. Dunnam, the Church was only twenty-seven years old and Dr. Dunnam was its third pastor, having been preceded by Dr. Charles W. Grant and Dr. J. Harold Beaty. Dr. Dunnam postulated that his new congregation was:

. . . in a unique position to become a dynamic force in the community. I see this in terms of the size of the congregation, its vision of its ministry, its willingness to address the vital issues affecting the lives of people in the city.

A native of Deemer, Mississippi, Dr. Dunnam graduated from the University of Southern Mississippi, Hattiesburg, Mississippi with a Bachelor of Arts degree and from Emory University in Atlanta with a Master of Theology degree. The Doctor of Divinity degree was conferred upon him by Asbury Theological Seminary in Wilmore, Kentucky. His previous pastorates have included Gulfport, Mississippi, Anaheim, California, San Clemente, California and Atlanta, Georgia. Mrs. Dunnam, Jerry, is a talented artist and was an illustrator for *Pockets*, a children's magazine; she also narrated some of the stories. She and Dr. Dunnam are the parents of three children, Kim, Kerry, and Kevin. They live at 3550 Central Avenue in Memphis.

Dr. Dunnam preached his first sermon as Pastor of Christ Church on March 28, 1982. In his introductory remarks, he quoted Sir Isaac Newton: "If we see further and understand more, it is because we have stood on shoulders of giants." Dr. Dunnam paid tribute to the founding Pastor, Dr. Charles W. Grant, and to the marvelous leadership of his immediate predecessor, Dr. Harold Beaty. He felt himself standing on the shoulders of two giants as he became the third Senior Minister of the congregation. His sermon of the day was entitled, "Chosen By God," and he introduced it by talking about his family life in rural Mississippi:

My Dad didn't even go to high school, but I've met few people whose wisdom compared to Dad's, even though I've moved among the high and mighty of the land, and have associated with some of the brilliant people of the country. He's a simple man of very few words, but when he speaks about important things, people listen.

My Dad is proud of me. I'm his youngest son. He's proud of who I am far more than what I've accomplished. Dad knows about the books I've written. I think he has read them all. He knows to some degree the world-wide impact my ministry at the Upper Room has had. But he's not overly impressed with that.

When Jerry called my Mom and Dad to tell them of our decision to accept this call to Christ Church, his response was spontaneous: 'Well, I'm glad he's getting back to his original call.' No questions, no discussion about what this meant to my career, or what it meant economically, or what the children

Dr. and Mrs. Maxie D. Dunnam

thought about it—just his expression of the heart of it all—the Call of God in my life.

I've gotten dozens of telephone calls from all over the nation since the news went out that I was leaving the Upper Room—calls from Bishops and persons from all areas of the church's life—but none of them was as focused as Dad. None of them as perceptive of the heart of the matter and the kind of decision I was making—a decision of vocation—of call.

With that introduction to his sermon, Dr. Dunnam established not only his roots in the richness of a rural family from Mississippi, but also his appreciation for the simple wisdom of his father. He established further the fact that he was at Christ Church because at the core of his being he felt called. Then he went on to preach his sermon, "Chosen By God," using a text from Ephesians 1:14. The outline of the sermon was very simple: I, Chosen; II, Chosen by God; and III, Chosen For a Purpose. In the sermon, Dr. Dunnam made the strong point that the failure of the Church is due to the failure of lay Christians to be convinced that they are called; they have been called by God, and their Christian baptism is their ordination. There is a note that Dr. Dunnam constantly sounds—the priesthood of all believers—the fact that a congregation is a company of ministers, set apart by God to minister to the people around them, as well as to reach out in ministry to the city, to the state, to the nation, and to the world.

The arrival of Dr. Dunnam in Memphis immediately preceded Holy Week. He and Reverend Jerry Corlew conducted the noon-day services and the Maundy Thursday special communion service. We were blessed with Easter Banners made and designed by Mrs. Austin Trousdale and her mother, Mrs. Forrest Dowling, Jr. The attendance at the Easter services surpassed all previous records—an attendance of 2,538 was recorded at the worship services.

As we approach each anniversary of the founding of Christ Church, we are reminded of our commitment from the beginning to be a missionary and an outreach church. Christ Church was supporting missionaries before it owned buildings. Mr. and Mrs. Gordon Greathouse, missionaries to Brazil, were home on furlough and visited the Church and talked with many, many groups; the Dean Schowengerdts from Korea also visited in October 1982 and told of the great revival prevalent in Korea. We were visited by Dr. and Mrs. Allen Walker (Sir Allen and Lady Walker) of Sydney, Australia. Sir Allen heads the Department of World Evangelism for the World Methodist Council. Both spoke to the congregation and to various groups. In the Fellowship Hall, the United Methodist Women entertained Lady Walker with a reception and tea which included women from the entire city of Memphis.

At a meeting, Dr. Dunnam presented some principles of church growth which he was asked to share with the congregation: "They [the Churches] grow by prayer and by the guidance of the Holy Spirit, by making a deliberate commitment to grow and by doing hard planning and work necessary for growth." He reminded the Administrative Board that God had unquestionably called Christ Church into being, and that our present membership has been bequeathed a great legacy to which our present leadership must continue to adhere. Dr. Dunnam further contended that one of the primary instruments for church growth is the Sunday School. No congregation can be a continuing and growing church without a vital and growing Sunday School with the Bible being taught in a challenging way, and with persons experiencing an accepting fellowship of love and concern. One of the ways that congregations grow through the Sunday School is to provide classes for every age group as well as for special interest groups. Sunday Schools also grow by starting new classes, especially if others have reached an optimum size; classes do not thrive in crowded quarters. Sunday School classes should also have an evangelical appeal in addition to an educational understanding as their mission. With the background of the great need for growth in the Church through the Sunday School, and upon recommendation of the Feasibility Committee, it was voted unanimously to move "full steam ahead" with construction of the additional rooms to the Activities Building, which was to be renamed the "J. Harold Beaty Building." The excitement was so high that the meeting was closed with the singing of the Doxology.

Christ Church was recognized at Annual Conference and at Lake Junaluska, North Carolina for leading the Conference in not only the most new members joining the Church during the Conference year 1985, but also in having the most persons received into the Church on profession of faith. Dr. Wayne Lamb, the Staff Minister in Evangelism, who spent many hours visiting prospective members for the Church, was delegated to receive these awards for the Church. The *Courier* carried words of appreciation for Dr. Lamb and headlines exclaimed, "Wayne, We Salute You!"

Recognized in one of the Sunday Worship Services was Reverend Howard Rash. In nearly every congregation there are persons who can no longer attend the worship services, and in our congregation, it is Reverend Rash who maintains a close and continuous fellowship with these "At Home Members"; they deeply appreciate his ministry. The August 8, 1982 *Courier* printed heartfelt words of gratitude for Reverend Rash and for his services. The front page again shouted, "Howard, We Salute You!"

The membership shared with keen interest the visit made in 1983 by Dr. and Mrs. Dunnam to Estonia, one of the Republics that comprise what we call Russia. The Dunnams were in special services in the Capital City of Tallin behind the Iron Curtain. More people worship in the Methodist

Church in Tallin, Estonia than in any other Methodist Church in Estonia although, in membership, Methodism in Estonia is small. Estonia is the only Republic in Russia where there are Methodists. Dr. and Mrs. Dunnam also spent two days with East European Methodists in Hermut, East Germany, and then they went on to the Berlin Wall where they joined in a "Day of Prayer for the World." Another important event of an earlier journey in 1982 was for the Dunnams to join the Executive Committee of the World Methodist Council, for its annual meeting in Brussels, Belgium, where Dr. Dunnam was Chairman of the Program Committee for the World Methodist Council.

The Christ Church Confirmation Class made ninety-one bookmarks, adorned with Christian symbols and favorite Bible verses, to send with pictures and a letter to the Pastor, Reverend Kuum, of the Methodist Church in Tallin. We had messages from Bishop Edward L. Tullis and from Dr. Eddie Fox of the Board of Discipleship, relating how sad it was to see what had happened to the Christian Church in that part of the world. There has been no Living Church movement in Russia since the Communist Revolution. Five decades and many persecutions later, 85% of the Orthodox Churches and 98% of their Seminaries are closed. The World Day of Prayer took on special meaning for the Dunnams in 1983 as they stood at the Berlin Wall and prayed with Christians around the world.

New staff members were announced as well as new responsibilities named for others. Shirley Lynn was designated Director of Evangelism and Singles Ministry; Sandra Brady was assigned to assist Marvin Budd in developing programs to meet the needs of the congregation; Reverend Jerry Corlew continued as Executive Minister and assisted in expanding the teaching ministry; Marvin Budd continued to direct the Council on Ministries, Program planning, and Children and Adult Education. The search began for a Youth Director and everyone was delighted when it was announced that Reverend James Loftin would be joining the staff in June of 1983, as Director of Youth Ministry. He had been serving in this same position in the Central United Methodist Church of Meridian, Mississippi. He is a native of Jackson, Mississippi, and has had wide experience in youth ministries. He attended Millsaps College in Jackson and Mississippi State College in Starkville, Mississippi where he received a Bachelor of Arts degree in Sociology, and he is a graduate of Asbury Theological Seminary of Wilmore, Kentucky. His wife, Carolyn, is a native of Kosciusko, Mississippi. They have two children, Ashley and Jonathan. Don Sanford, who had been Minister of Music at Christ Church since 1970, resigned. He and his wife, Marjorie, had rendered excellent service in the Music Ministry and in the development of Children and Youth choirs. A reception and an appreciation dinner were given for them the last of September.

Immediately, the search began for a new Director of Music Ministries. After several months, announcement was made that Michael T. Brewster, would begin his Music Ministry on the staff early in 1983. Michael Brewster is a native of Cleveland, Tennessee. His Bachelor of Music Degree is from the Westminster Choir College, Princeton, New Jersey. He later received the Master of Music degree from Indiana University, which was awarded cum laude, with a major in Vocal Pedagogy. He came to Christ Church from a very successful ministry at the United Methodist Church at Haddenfield, New Jersey. Mike and his wife, Julie, who is also a musician, have two children, Scott and Lauren. They were warmly received by the congregation on May 6, 1983.

E. R. Richmond, Sr., Chairman of the Architect and Building Committee, gave a final report on the recent construction activity. Construction on the addition to the Activities Building was completed at a total cost of $693,762.73, which included the construction of the Utility Building, additional office space and paving of a parking lot. The other members of this Committee were Nancy Beasley, Don Bourland, Sewell Dunkin, Dr. Jim Eoff, Charlie Johnson, Ken Markwell, Jack Renshaw, Trudy Simpson and Judy Van Steenburg. Ed Thorn, Architect, shared some thoughts with us in his report.

In Mini-Conferences, the leaders were Dr. Randall Crandall, Director of Evangelism with the Board of Discipleship in Nashville, and Dr. Robert Tuttle, Lecturer and Professor with Oral Roberts University School of Theology. Dr. Tuttle is one of the founders of the Board of the United Methodist Renewal Services Fellowship.

At Annual Conference in June 1983, Reverend Jerry Corlew who had served as Executive Minister for the past five years was appointed to be the pastor of Collierville United Methodist Church, Collierville, Tennessee. Dr. Dunnam announced the appointment of Reverend Earl A. Johnston as the new Executive Minister. Reverend Johnston came to Christ Church from the position of District Superintendent of the Paducah District. He holds a Master of Divinity degree from Memphis Theological Seminary. He and his wife, Jerry, are the parents of two children, Philip and Suzanne, both grown and married.

One of the "Spiritual Dividends" that has come to Memphis with the leadership of Dr. and Mrs. Dunnam is the "Walk to Emmaus." It is an effective model of renewal and growth developed by the Board of Discipleship, through *The Upper Room* when Dr. Dunnam was the World Editor. The Emmaus Walk centers in the theology of Grace—God's unmerited love offered to all. The goal is inspiration, renewal and challenge for persons to live out the Christian faith through their church and in their community. It is a seventy-two hour conference in a retreat-type setting, beginning on a Thursday evening and closing on Sunday evening. During the weekend, persons listen to talks by clergy and laity on themes from the Christian life, share together in small table groups, pray together and celebrate Holy Communion. The Gospel story of the Emmaus Walk (Luke 24:13-35) is the example of this Conference. Jesus walked with the disciples on the Road to Emmaus, opened the Scripture to them, and was revealed to them in the breaking of bread. The Emmaus Walk, although started in Memphis by Christ Church, is now an Ecumenical Ministry. Persons from Second Presbyterian, Decatur-Trinity Christian, Lindenwood Christian, Bellevue Baptist, Central Church, Calvary and St. Mary's Episcopal Churches, and a number of other churches have been involved.

A Preaching Mission with Dr. Lloyd Ogilvie of First Presbyterian Church, Hollywood, California, as the speaker, was a spiritual feature of the fall season. He appears weekly on a nationally televised program, entitled, "Let God Love You," in which he seeks to help people turn their struggles into stepping-stones. Through the years, Christ Church has had the good fortune, at the invitation of its ministers, to hear some of the truly great preachers of our age. Listed are some who have visited and spoken:

Bishop Marvin Franklin	Dr. Ben Johnson
Bishop H. E. Finger, Jr.	Dr. Kermit Long
Bishop Earl G. Hunt	Dr. Jordan Grooms
Bishop Edward L. Tullis	Dr. Charles Allen
Bishop William R. Cannon	Dr. James Buskirk
Bishop Joel McDavid	Dr. Elton Trueblood
Bishop Frank Robinson	Dr. Arnold Prater
Bishop Robert Goodrich	Dr. Lawrence Lacour
Bishop Ernest Fitzgerald	Dr. Bill Starnes
Bishop Ernest W. Newman	Dr. Charles Swindoll
Dr. Wallace Hamilton	Sir Allen Walker and
Dr. Ralph W. Sockman	Lady Walker
Dr. Harry Denman	Dr. Robert Tuttle
Dr. J. Manning Potts	Dr. Randall Crandall
Dr. Fred Pfisterer	Dr. Eddie Fox
	Dr. James T. Laney

In closing the year 1983, it was noticed that for the third consecutive year, the church budget projections exceeded one million dollars. This was the second consecutive year, following the "Every Member Canvass," that the amount pledged was over and above the suggested budget.

A sad time of this year was the date of death of Sandra Brady on June 14th, after a long and valiant fight with cancer. Sandra and Dale Brady had been such a vital part of the Activities Program from the very beginning when the

Activities Building was completed and opened for use. Her latest assignment was to assist Marvin Budd in the area of Program.

Later, the last of November 1983, the saddened Church and community suffered the loss of Mary Anna Grant, wife of Dr. Charles W. Grant, the founding minister of Christ Church. She, too, suffered a long illness; but she was forever triumphant in her life of service.

In Dr. Dunnam's Report to the Charge Conference at the close of 1984, are these statements: "1984 has been one of the most exciting years of my ministry, and I believe one of the most exciting years in the magnificent history of Christ United Methodist Church."

Christ Church has amassed an outstanding staff. Significant changes have been made to increase the effectiveness of the Church's ministry. The Executive Minister, Reverend Earl Johnston, includes in his responsibilities that of Pastoral Care. This became possible because of the addition of a part-time Business Manager, Henry Hottum, who is rendering outstanding service in this area. Donna Thomas who had been the assistant to Dale Brady in the Activities Program, was named Director of Recreation Ministries, following his resignation. The ministry involved 19,000 persons during the current year and included a variety of activities.

The Christ Church Day School acquired a new Director, David Fox, who was employed following the resignation of Sam Drash. The Day School continued to enjoy a fine reputation for excellent training and quality education. From Kindergarten through the Sixth Grade the enrollment at present is 410 pupils, with 150 children enrolled in the "Parent's Day Out Program," which is also under the auspices of the Day School.

Perhaps one of the most urgent and dramatic needs that has been addressed, was the establishment of a Counseling and Family Life Center, staffed by a trained professional. Reverend Ed Horton was asked to head this important ministry. During this time Mrs. Earl Johnston (Jerry) was secretary for the Counseling Center. The Counseling Center was housed in the larger cottage at 4448 Poplar at the corner of Poplar Avenue and East Cherry Circle.

The membership of Christ Church continues to grow, in spite of the kind of mobile society that we have in the nation as well as in the city. The Church must receive 300 members to show a net gain of 100 members. At present, our membership statistics stand at 3,739, the largest number of members on roll thus far in the history of the Church. For the year 1984, Christ Church received into its fellowship 237 members with 110 of those being received on profession of faith.

The goal of striving to have fifty percent of our income go for Missions and Outreach Ministries has been present in the life and thinking of Christ Church from the very beginning. Currently, it appears that we have spent about thirty-nine percent of our income for these ministries, and during the next year, the percentage will reach approximately forty-one percent. One of the glorious expressions of Outreach Ministry is the manner in which Christ Church has supported Methodist Neighborhood Centers. For a number of years the Church has provided full-time support for Mr. Franklin Perry, who has been our Inner-City Missionary, rendering ministries and services in North Memphis. Only eternity can measure the full impact of this Christ-centered work. Recently another dimension was added to the Methodist Neighborhood Centers by augmenting and supporting another staff member, Reverend Billy Joe Jackson. His primary task is Evangelism and the development of a community of faith, perhaps leading to the establishment of a new congregation in connection with the Centers. Our Church has been selected by the Board of Discipleship to share in launching a Prison Ministry, nationwide. Charles Colson's visit to our Church was of great assistance in launching and establishing this vital ministry. The last General Conference urged Methodist Churches to become involved in this desperate area of concern.

Sunday School growth was visible by the organization of two new Sunday School classes. These classes were for adults and each has approximately twenty-five members making a total of fifty new adults in Sunday School. The names of the classes are "Positive Christian Married" and "Logos."

In the Small Group Ministry it is significant that 209 adults were involved in a six-weeks study of *The Workbook on Spiritual Disciplines*. These groups and other groups continue in study following the Fellowship Dinners on each Wednesday evening. There is a keen interest in Bible Study and in topics for spiritual information and enrichment.

Dr. Dunnam has emphasized over and over again that we must provide the most outstanding ministry possible for our children and young people. His emphasis has also been placed on our being bold in our proposals of ministries that we as a congregation can provide for the needs of this great city. These duties and privileges demand our imagination, energy, time and financial resources and dare us to be creative in seeking where we can make a difference in the world and in the lives of people.

Throughout this entire year of 1984, there was a song of celebration as Methodism observed its 200th birthday. In May of this year, General Conference went back to the city of Baltimore, Maryland, for their Quadrennial Meeting and especially they visited "Lovely Lane Chapel" (restored) on the spot where the Christmas Conference of 1784 met and where the organization of the Methodist Church in America took place. During all of 1984, sermons have been preached, programs have been presented, classes and seminars on Methodism have been offered, and drama and music have brought inspiration to thousands of Methodists. We have not only relived our history and heritage, but we have set new goals for a more effective ministry as we hear again the clarion call of "Offer Them Christ" by John Wesley, which led Frances Asbury and Thomas Coke to come to America.

Traditionally, Protestants have made little use of visual art in their churches. Kenneth Wyatt's "Offer Them Christ" has opened up for us a new dimension in Christian art. This new epic painting of John Wesley sending Thomas Coke to America is historically accurate and is deepening our inspiration and motivation for Evangelism at every level of Methodism. This painting was first unveiled at the Congress on Evangelism, January 1984 and later introduced to the General Conference to inspire Church leaders at all levels to be challenged as never before by John Wesley's great commission for spreading the Gospel to America. The Foundation for Evangelism has made copies of this painting available for use in local churches. In keeping with the Bicentennial, Dr. and Mrs. Wayne A. Lamb presented to Christ Church a framed copy of this painting, "Offer Them Christ." It hangs in the east corridor beside the Sanctuary.

Complying with Methodist tradition, Christ Church celebrated the Bicentennial with a series of sermons on our faith by Dr. Dunnam. Reverend Earl Johnston taught a course on Methodism following the Fellowship Dinners on Wednesday nights. We have sung many of the Wesley hymns, and the choir joined with other choirs of the city to present an evening of special music and narration of our history. This same choral group was invited to share this program at the Bicentennial Annual Conference, meeting in Jackson, Tennessee in the Civic Center. As a part of the celebration, General Conference set a goal for Methodism to double its membership by 1992.

Christmas 1984 was a thrilling and climactic celebration. Not only was the Christmas Eve "Come and Go Communion" observed by families and friends from five to seven o'clock in the evening, but a relatively new tradition was initiated with the Candlelight/Carol Service beginning at 10:30 p.m. on that same evening. Under the leadership of Mike Brewster, Director of Music Ministries, many new features were added: Orchestra, New Covenant Singers, Senior High Vocal Ensemble and a Living Nativity. The Procession of Lights began at 11:00 p.m., with the combined choirs entering the Sanctuary carrying lighted candles and singing, "O Come All Ye Faithful." Simultaneously, the Christ candle of the Advent wreath was lighted, signifying that we are in the last hour of preparation before the birth and Advent of Jesus. There was the reading of the Christmas story both from the Gospel of Matthew and from the Gospel of Luke, followed by the singing of the carols appropriate to these Scriptures. Especial moments of this service were during the arrival of Mary and Joseph with their new-born son, Jesus, and during the presentation of the Christmas message, "The Perfect Gift," by Dr. Dunnam. In closing the service, the congregation stood and sang "Silent Night, Holy Night," lifting high their candles signifying that the true Light of God has come to earth.

The New Year 1985 began well with a called session of the Charge Conference to recommend Ronald B. Thomas, Jr. as a candidate for the ordained ministry. Ron is a student in Candler School of Theology, Emory University, Atlanta, Georgia.

Early in the year, the members of the Steering Committee who labored such long hours and with such commitment to launch the new church in East Memphis, later to be named Christ Church, were made Honorary Members of the Administrative Board. The following persons became our first Honorary Members: James H. Seabrook, Sr., H. L. Davenport, E. C. Handorf, Fred M. Ridolphi, Samuel H. Mays, C. R. McDaniel, Dr. W. J. Templeton and Lee B. McCormick.

The children of our Music Makers and Young Musicians Choirs presented a colorful program on Sunday afternoon May 5, 1985, entitled, "Back at the Creekbank," under the direction of Mike Brewster, who played the part of Mr. Jenkins. Through dialogue and song some great truths were spoken by the children: "When I look at the wonderful world He's made, I know God must love me." And "God paints the world with love, that's how I know He lives."

Recently a beautiful Altar Dossal was presented for the Christ Church Chapel in honor of Reverend Howard W. Rash. This work of art in needlepoint was designed and executed by Mr. Charles Roma assisted by Mrs. Mary Kelley, Mrs. Dorothy Stafford, Mrs. Edith Middlecoff and Mrs. Frances Roberts. It represents more than 2000 hours of loving labor. It contains symbols of our Triumphant Lord and is surrounded by panels depicting the Ministry of Christ and His Church.

The Thirtieth Anniversary of Christ United Methodist Church was celebrated in a special way on Sunday, June 16, 1985 with a visit from our new Bishop, Bishop Ernest W. Newman, who preached at both the worship services. In the late afternoon in the Courtyard of the Church, the Annual Picnic was held which included games and contests for the children and young people, and fellowship and singing for the entire group of members and visitors. During the year, there will be other events to observe the Thirtieth Anniversary; for example, the publication of a *History* of these first thirty years is planned.

Christ Church has moved into another area of Mission by serving as host to a pilot project involving Prison Fellowship Ministry, Habitat for Humanity and World Vision. This "Trinity Project," as it is being called, is the first of its kind in the nation. Habitat for Humanity is a world-wide builder of houses for low-income families. Six minimum security prison inmates who are professing Christians will be housed by volunteer families to engage in meaningful work experiences and develop vocational skills as they build or restore homes for impoverished citizens who do not have the resources to build or repair their homes. Shelby County Mayor Bill Morris has estimated that there are 38,000 vacant substandard housing units in our city. We can make a difference.

Another exciting ministry was realized with the announcement by the Staff-Parish Relations Committee that Fred Mills is to be Coordinator of Local Missions and Outreach Ministries. Fred will be a full-time volunteer and will serve on the staff without pay. He has felt the call of God in his life for some time and took early retirement so that he could devote full time to this ministry. He is coordinating the Habitat for Humanity Project, and will coordinate the Jubilee Ministries outlined by the Council on Ministries. This will include work with the many ministries at the United Methodist Neighborhood Centers.

Communication is inadequate to share on paper the way in which God is working in and through the great Church he commissioned through the hopes and dreams of dedicated laymen and laywomen in June 1955—known to us as Christ United Methodist Church.

Clergy 1985
Dr. Maxie D. Dunnam, center; left to right, Reverend Howard W. Rash; Dr. Wayne A.
Lamb; Reverend Earl. A. Johnston; Reverend James L. Loftin.

United Methodist Women

*Go ye therefore, and teach all nations, baptizing them in the name of
the Father, and of the Son, and of the Holy Ghost:
Teaching them to observe all things whatsoever I have commanded
you: and, lo, I am with you always, even unto the end of the world.*
— Mark 28:19, 20 (KJV)

It is impossible to express in words the full impact that Methodist women
have had across the years in helping to build the Kingdom of God not only
here but also around the world. It was not long after the middle of the 19th
century that the General Conferences of the various branches of Methodism
authorized the forming of Women's Missionary Societies. Already women
had unofficial groups to raise money and render services to the needy, both
at home and overseas. It seems that from the very beginning, women had a
special concern and compassion for helping other women and children,
whether here in our communities, or in China, or in India and other countries. Schools and hospitals were established, as well as churches, to minister
and to improve the quality of life in the true spirit of Christ.

According to the history recorded in *The Spreading Flame* (the history of
the missionary work of our Methodist women in the Memphis Conference),
the first Women's Missionary Society was organized in this Conference in
1878 at Brownsville, Tennessee, and the Memphis Conference Women's
Missionary Society was organized here in Memphis in April of 1879 at First
Methodist Church. It is also significant, as well as important, that shortly
after the organization of Christ Methodist Church, June 26, 1955, the women
met to organize the local units of the Woman's Society of Christian Service

and the Wesleyan Service Guild.

The Committee for organization was as follows:

Mrs. Charles M. Henderson	Madison Heights
Mrs. Hugh Carey	Madison Heights
Mrs. Percy Whitenton	First Church
Mrs. J. C. Ingram	First Church
Mrs. Thomas West	St. John's
Mrs. Richard Taylor	St. John's
Mrs. Oscar Crofford	Trinity
Mrs. F. M. Ridolphi	Trinity
Mrs. J. V. Thomas	St. Luke's
Mrs. H. C. Shelton	St. Luke's

This Committee met on June 28, 1955, and selected officers to be elected to serve for the first year of the organization:

President, Mrs. Percy Whitenton
Vice President, Mrs. Charles M. Henderson
Secretary, Mrs. Jack Caskey
Treasurer, Mrs. Horace Harwell
Assistant Treasurer, Mrs. W. K. Martak

Secretary of:
Promotion, Mrs. Ned French
Missionary Education, Mrs. Clarence Colby
Christian Social Relations and Local Church Activities,
    Mrs. Fred Ridolphi
Spiritual Life, Mrs. W. J. Templeton
Student Work, Mrs. Sam Mays
Youth Work, Mrs. Charles Tate
Children's Work, Mrs. J. C. Ingram, Jr.
Literature and Publications, Mrs. Ray Drenner
Supplies, Mrs. Edgar Tenent
Status of Women, Mrs. Jack Byrne

The Circle Leaders:

1. Mrs. Howard Davenport	5. Mrs. Ernest Felts
2. Mrs. Richard Taylor	6. Mrs. Ed Richmond, Sr.
3. Mrs. Russell Reeves	7. Mrs. Merle King
4. Mrs. Robert Holt	8. Mrs. John Parsons

9. Mrs. J. T. Canfield   11. Mrs. D. K. Kelley
10. Mrs. Hugh Carey

The Wesleyan Service Guild Officers:

Chairman, Mrs. Porter McClean
Vice Chairman, Mrs. Haskell Gass
Secretary, Miss Zetta Walker
Treasurer, Miss Agnes Thomas
Secretary of Promotion, Mrs. Floyd Dixon

Mrs. Percy Whitenton (Ethel) had been a very active and capable worker
in First Methodist Church. It was her goal to set up the organization of the
Woman's Society of Christian Service and the Wesleyan Service Guild at
Christ Church according to the guidelines set forth in *The Handbook* so that
each member would be able to share in the opportunities for fellowship and
growth in wisdom, understanding, and in her relationship to God. At the
meeting, 157 women became Charter Members. Later the report reached
215. Mrs. Whitenton and her husband worked tirelessly and as a team in
many of the activities in the early life of the Church. She served for some
years as Parish Visitor and with her warm and loving personality brought
many new families into the congregation. She was a radiant beam of sunshine
to the shut-ins whom she visited. Ethel Whitenton was a very creative person;
one of the examples of her creativity was the Chrismon Tree. She was not
only the originator of the idea, but also the driving force behind the project,
making many of the ornaments herself. Another example of her creative
genius and the sharing of her talent was the designing and making of the
beautiful Casket Pall to be used in funerals.

The second President of the Woman's Society of Christian Service was
Mrs. Fred M. Ridolphi (Rinne) and along with her, serving as Chairman of
the Wesleyan Service Guild, was Mrs. Haskell Gass (Ruby). The scope of
the work, along with the membership, continued to grow. The women were
not only busy making and paying their pledges to Missions, both foreign
and home, but there were many places in the life of the new Christ Church
that needed the services of teaching, telephoning, visiting, preparing countless meals for Church dinners, and preparing sandwiches and snacks for the
children and youth programs. Mrs. Ridolphi was a member of the Committee on History and under the leadership of Mrs. W. J. Templeton (Elizabeth)
as Chairman, she along with Mrs. Ethel Whitenton kept important records
for the History of the Church.

The third President of the Woman's Society was Mrs. Clarence Colby
(Margaret), who has the distinction of serving as president of the Woman's

Society on two different occasions. The first term was 1957-58, and a later term was 1969-70. The Chairman of the Wesleyan Service Guild for this first term was Mrs. V. A. Alexander (Bernice). Margaret Colby had grown up in a Methodist Parsonage home, being the daughter of Dr. and Mrs. John L. Horton, so it may be concluded that she was well-schooled in Methodism and the work of Methodist women. During the beginning, when the church services were held at the Plaza Theater, she and Mrs. Grant served as Greeters and welcomed the people as they came to the worship services. The Wesleyan Service Guild was named for Margaret and was known always as the Margaret Colby Wesleyan Service Guild.

In 1958, Mrs. Ernest Felts (Helen) became President of United Methodist Women and was the first person to serve for two years, concluding her term in 1960. During this time, there were two persons who served as Chairmen of the Wesleyan Service Guild. They were Mrs. Sanford L. Jones and Miss Zetta Walker. One of the highlights of those years was the beautiful Membership Teas in which the Woman's Society honored their new members.

Those were the days before there was a kitchen staff, so the women served many of the meals. One of the big events each month was the serving of the dinner for the Methodist Men. Before the Fellowship Hall was built and in the summertime, some of these meals were served on the lawn at the Cottage.

Just as the Church began with a missionary emphasis, so the Woman's Society gave undaunted support to the work of Wesley House, a Home Missions project begun in North Memphis in 1906, and the Bethlehem Center, a similar project begun in 1935 serving the Black Community in South Memphis and located on Walker Avenue. Mrs. Charles M. Henderson (Mary) was a member of the Board of Missions and the Woman's Division. She was a member of both Boards of these two ministries until her death in 1968. The women of Christ Church had key women and other members of the Woman's Society and the Wesleyan Service Guild who attended the Board meetings regularly and kept the groups informed and in active participation, by giving many services and supplies to meet the needs of these institutions as they served these areas of the city. In 1968, the Boards of these institutions were consolidated and their ministries merged under the direction of the United Methodist Neighborhood Centers.

Another mission project, begun in 1966, was the Reelfoot Rural Ministry, located in Lake County, Tennessee, an area that has been blighted by people being unable to find work; these persons have been displaced by machines that cultivate and harvest the cotton and other crops. This ministry has received the support of the total Church as well as the support of the Woman's Society. Regularly they need food, clothes, money and items for conducting classes and recreation programs and for other ministries.

On the Executive Committee each year, there is a "Key Woman" for the

Methodist Hospital Auxiliary. This representative and members from the circles carry suggested items to meet the needs in the Love Ward and other areas of the Hospitals. The membership to the Methodist Hospital Auxiliary is one dollar per year for each woman, and great emphasis is placed on one hundred precent membership for each group of the United Methodist Women.

Christ Church women's groups cooperate with Church Women United, a city-wide organization of the women from all churches in the City, including all denominations. They meet once each month and, on an ecumenical basis, minister to many needs locally. One of their ministries is to the prisoners in the jails. In 1976 the women of Christ Church began saving books, magazines and other items in order to assist and cooperate in this service to others.

Another Community service is participation in the Reading is Fundamental Program (R.I.F.). This is a government program to provide books for children in the city schools that are unable to buy books for reading. It is a matching project and the women of Christ Church are assigned to work with LaRose School.

Each year, beginning in 1953, the women of Memphis Conference give to a Scholarship Fund at Lambuth College. The income from this increasing fund is used to assist in the education of deserving students, preference being given young women planning to enter full-time Christian service under the auspices of the Women's Division of the Board of Global Ministries. An offering is taken each year as well as an item is designated in the budget to support this scholarship.

It was an exciting event when in 1967 the Woman's Society of Christ Church entertained the Annual Meeting of the Memphis Conference Woman's Society and Wesleyan Service Guild. Mrs. James B. Green was the Conference President. This was one of the ways we celebrated the opening of the Sanctuary and the sharing of Christ Church with others. The visitors from all over the Memphis Conference were welcomed to Christ Church by the pastor, Dr. Charles W. Grant, the president of the Woman's Society, Mrs. O. B. Crofford (Bea) and Mrs. Howard Estes (Lorice), Chairman of the Wesleyan Service Guild. The theme of this Annual Meeting was, "In Thy Light We Walk." We were honored to have on the program Dr. James S. Wilder, Jr., President of Lambuth College, Mrs. H. M. Russell (Frankie), President of the Southeastern Jurisdiction Woman's Society of Christian Service and Dr. James T. Laney, Professor in the Divinity School of Vanderbilt University, who later became President of Emory University, Atlanta, Georgia.

The Women also participated in many services when the Memphis Annual Conference, which includes all the ministers and the lay persons who represent the various churches, met at Christ Church in June of 1965. Bishop Homer Ellis Finger, Jr. was in his first year as a new Bishop and presided over the sessions. From the very beginning of the history of Christ Church and the Woman's Society of Christian Service and United Methodist Women, the members of these organizations have been both gracious and generous in entertaining Conference, District and community meetings whenever it has been requested.

A hundred years ago the women's organization was "The Woman's Missionary Society." Later and for a short period, this organization became two groups, "The Woman's Foreign Missionary Society" and "The Woman's Home Missionary Society." There was even a third group known as "The Ladies' Aid Society"; however, their work consisted mostly of looking after the parsonages. Then in 1940, after the union in 1939 of the three branches of Methodism, when we became "The Methodist Church," the name of the women's organization was changed to the "Woman's Society of Christian Service" and a "Wesleyan Service Guild" for professional and employed women. These organizations for women continued until 1972, when the Women's Division changed the name to "United Methodist Women" and we moved into one inclusive organization. These events remind us of a quotation that we used frequently from the *A-Guide* of 1940:

> Nothing is permanent except change. But God has endowed us with a capacity to face the new and untried because change is a part of His creative plan and purpose. Throughout the centuries the Christian Church has confronted change, as cultures, conditions and needs have brought new concepts of life. In the light of history we would be craven cowards to fear change. Rather, we would sing with the Psalmist, 'This is the day which the Lord hath made, we will rejoice and be glad in it.'

Statistics tell us that almost half of the women in our nation have entered the working world and are either employed or pursuing careers. This has created some serious obstacles in the number of Methodist women able to participate in the meetings and programs of the United Methodist Women. Yet the organization of United Methodist Women in Christ Church has an enrollment of 473 with seventeen Circles or Groups. Two of these Groups meet at night and are designed for the employed and career woman. In 1980, the President and Executive Committee initiated the use of "Service Circles" which have succeeded, and the plan has even been followed by other churches in the Conference. These four Service Groups are:

Group 12 . . . . Church Service Group
Group 13 . . . . Neighborhood Centers
Group 14 . . . . Wesley-Highland Manor
Group 15 . . . . Membership and Visitation

The purpose of these Service Groups is exactly what the name implies. They minister to the Church, providing needed services, articles, supplies as needed; to the Neighborhood Centers in its mission to the needy; to the Wesley-Highland Manor, a nursing home for the infirm and elderly, where loving concern is a priceless service; and to the ministry of visitation and cultivation of new and prospective members and a ministry to the shut-ins. In all of the seventeen Groups, there is a Leader and a Study Leader. The Groups meet the first Tuesday of each month except July and August. When the business of each group is transacted then the Study Leader conducts the Bible Study on the topic designated by the Women's Division for that year.

A project that involved more than sixty women, most of them from the United Methodist Women's organization of the Church, was begun in 1975 — the project of the Needlepoint Kneeling Cushions for the Sanctuary. This involved an estimated 39,000 hours of needlework and 6,379,408 stitches. The Kneeling Chsions were completed and dedicated on May 28, 1978 "To the Glory of God and of His Kingdom."

One of the exciting events that has been initiated in recent years is the Annual Fellowship Day. It began as a part of the Mission Study Series in 1981 and was used to carry out the theme of the Study with music, program and food. It has also been observed as a time of fun and relaxation with a luncheon in a lovely spacious home.

We wish it were possible to list the names of each person who has rendered loving service, but the names on the list are innumerable, and many names are only known to the Angels in Heaven, so we simply say, "Thank you and God bless you."

A Dream Becomes A Reality: Christ Methodist Day School

Remember now thy Creator in the days of thy youth...
— Ecclesiastes 12:1 (KJV)

Suffer little children, and forbid them not, to come unto me: for of such is the kingdom of heaven.
— Matthew 19:14 (KJV)

It began as a dream. A dream which would grow and flourish and touch many lives. A dream of high hopes, high ideals and high standards. This dream came true as Christ Methodist Day School.

In 1955 soon after the Church was organized the Commission on Education with Harry A. Johnson, Jr. as Chairman, studied the need for a School. It was decided to begin with a kindergarten in the fall of 1958. This was readily accepted by the Official Board. In the first year, seventy-five pupils were enrolled in three classes; the faculty consisted of two full-time teachers, Mrs. Charles McVean and Mrs. A. A. Sippel. Mrs. James Curry was hired as a teacher trainee. The tuition was established at $12.50 per month per student. Harry Johnson stressed from the very beginning that this Day School was established to provide the finest Kindergarten program possible for the children and would be conducted by thoroughly qualified Christian teachers. To this day, it has never wavered from this ideal and standard.

Mrs. McVean was named the Director of the Day School and oversaw the first fifteen years of its growth and development. Because of her many years of tireless effort and her dedication to high standards, Christ Methodist Day School is recognized as one of the finest institutions providing Christian education in our city.

By 1960 the need for expansion was recognized, thus the first grade and a program for four-year-olds were added. From 1961 to 1965, one section of one new grade was added through the sixth grade. The first class of sixth graders was graduated on May 17, 1966. Each year from 1968 through 1978 an additional section of each grade was added and in 1971 a program for three-year-olds was begun. At this time Christ Methodist Day School maintained thirteen pre-school classes and eleven grade school classes, involving over 380 children.

When Mrs. McVean retired in June of 1974, Sam Drash was employed as Director. Through his encouragement, guidance and love, the Day School continued to maintain its high ideals of growth and development. From the first day of its inception, the Day School has been an integral part of the Church's ministry. There has been the firm belief that each person is one of God's children and Christ Methodist Day School is committed to helping each student develop his or her full potential academically, physically, socially, emotionally and spiritually. In fact, this last statement has become the statement of purpose for the school.

In the booklet prepared for the Twenty-fifth Anniversary Celebration there is a story entitled "The Faith and Prayers of One Person are Realized." This story has a beautiful relation to the history of the Day School. It is the story of a dream of a small girl and how it came true almost forty years later. The story goes thus:

> In the midst of a serious illness, this little girl had a dream in which God visited her. He beckoned her to come home with Him, but she insisted that she had many things to do on this earth. After much discussion, she and God struck an agreement — that she would remain on earth and everything she would do with her life would be for the Lord. This little girl recovered from her illness and earnestly set out to achieve this goal. We know her as our own Ella McVean.

The story continued to say that very early in life, Mrs. McVean began her work with children. While still in high school she became an aide in a kindergarten class and after her graduation she taught a year in a country school. She soon realized that she needed more preparation, so she attended college and then taught four years before her marriage. After her marriage, Charles McVean's work took him to many places along the Mississippi River. This meant for them many moves, but wherever they lived, they always found a church home and Mrs. McVean continued to carry out her promise to the Lord and to work with children. Through her love and work, her dream took shape and grew. When Charles McVean's work brought him to

Memphis and the family settled here, they began to attend St. John's Methodist Church. Here again, Ella McVean became a dedicated worker with kindergarten children in the ministry of the Church. All of her life she had loved and enjoyed music and she was able to share her musical talent as she nurtured the young children in her care. Even as she worked, she was dreaming of having someday a Christian school and was storing ideas for her later pursuits.

About this time the city of Memphis began to expand to the east. The McVeans were aware of this and began thinking about a new church home. Soon they heard the good news that a new Methodist Church was being organized on Poplar Avenue, somewhere between Highland and Perkins. That new church was soon to be known as Christ Methodist Church. It was already well known that Mrs. McVean was an excellent worker with children so she was called on to organize the nursery program at this new Church.

It is a truly modern mission story; she began with no equipment save twelve apple boxes and very little space in the Poplar Plaza Theater. However, as she loved and cared for the children, the number grew from Sunday to Sunday and soon a temporary building was provided. She and her family arrived at 8:00 a.m. each Sunday morning to set up the arrangements and prepare for the arrival of the Nursery children, only to have to dismantle it at the close of the service for the theater use.

As a member of the Work Area on Education, Mrs. McVean and others saw the need for a Christian school for boys and girls in the area of the new Church. After two years of discussion of this need, a Day Kindergarten was approved—the dreams of her life were beginning to come true. Because of her concern and intense interest, she resigned her position at another school and spent all of the 1957-58 school year planning for the new school. To begin she had two classrooms and two teachers besides herself. Also, the plan was that the school was to be self-supporting and that she, as Director, was to report directly to the Official Board, or Administrative Board of the Church, as it is now called.

The Christ Church Day School opened in September 1958 with three teachers and an enrollment of seventy-five pupils. From that day, the school has grown to be recognized as one of the finest educational institutions in the city of Memphis, always maintaining a Christian atmosphere. The school could not have arrived at its present pinnacle of success had it not been for the dedication and hard work of Mrs. McVean and those who served her. There were times when she served not only as Director, but also as teacher, bookkeeper, purchasing manager, nurse, nutritionist, counselor, curriculum director and sometimes coordinator of maintenance. It was a monumental task for anyone, but this was the realization of her dream come true—the glorification of the Heavenly Father and helping young children to grow in

His love.

After Mrs. McVean retired as Director of the Christ Methodist Day School in June 1974, the Board of Directors employed Sam L. Drash. In the brochure-booklet printed for the Twenty-fifth Anniversary, there are many cherished pictures of the early beginnings as well as pictures of the success and growth of the school. Among these are the names and pictures of some of the dedicated faculty and others who gave untiringly of their services. In addition to Mrs. McVean there were:

Mrs. Janet Templeton	Mrs. Joyce Bruno
Mrs. J. A. Carson	Mrs. Dorothy J. Lewis
Mrs. Ann Curry	Miss Linda McVean
Mrs. O. F. Gibson	Miss D'Ann Sullivan
Mrs. A. A. Sippel	Mrs. James East
Mrs. Emma Dillon	Mrs. Allison Herron
Mrs. Ernie Leachman	Mrs. Don Finnel
Mr. Sam Drash	Mrs. Lloyd Ashley
Mrs. Dorris Smith	Mrs. Roy Greenlee
Mrs. Flicky Hartman	Mrs. Lucian Wadlington
Mrs. Mary Ann Dilling	Miss Mary Ann Stevens

At intervals, the Chairman of the Board of the Christ Church Day School and the Director presented reports of the progress and work of the Day School. The September 1969 Report contained the following information:

The School is operating at almost full capacity. There is a quota of eighteen students per class and fourteen of the seventeen classes have their quota. The total enrollment at present is 294 with a maximum capacity of 306 students. This is the maximum enrollment which we have experienced. The growth of the enrollment for the past few years is:

1965-66	239
1966-67	247
1967-68	269
1968-69	294

Although our fees may be lower than other private schools, they were raised in 1968 and commitments have been made for the current year. There are no other fees; parents pay extra for tests. The school owns many of the textbooks used. All new ones will be bought by the students this year. The students bring their own lunches and buy milk at cost.

Since each of the ten kindergarten classes meet for only half a day, only twelve classrooms are needed to accommodate the seventeen classes. The School uses two additional rooms—one for the Office and one for the Library.

The curriculum includes:

Mathematics	Spelling	Science
Reading	Language	Art
Writing	Social Studies	Music
French	Physical Education	

In September 1969 the School increased its monthly payment to the Church from $175 to $200 for the nine months that the School is in session. There were 214 students enrolled who are not mem- of Christ Church. The students that come from other churches are as follows:

Other Methodist	39
Presbyterian	54
Baptist	35
Episcopal	37
Catholic	26
Jewish	3
Other Faiths	20
Total	214

Sam Drash came to the position as Director of Christ Church Day School from St. Petersburg, Florida. He had graduated from Southwestern in Memphis (now Rhodes College) in 1961 with a Bachelor of Arts degree and a major in History. He received a Masters degree in Education and later a second Masters degree from Auburn University in Alabama. He is married to the former Virginia Taylor of Como, Mississippi, and they have three sons—Lewis, Michael, and Wayne.

A report from the Day School Committee given by Ed Richmond, Sr. in January 1975, referred to the School's being sixteen years old. At this time, the school had a budget of $192,850 and was not subsidized by the Church; in fact, $7,000 a year is paid to the Church to cover expenses. The enrollment was 390 pupils and all students are considered above average. All the facilities meet the standards of the City Board of Education and the State Welfare Department. All teachers are certified and the emphasis is always on religious training. Sam Drash made regular reports to the Administrative Board as well as to the Board of Directors of the Day School. The report given at the time the Day School was observing the Twenty-fifth Anniversary is a valid summary of the work done. This is dated October 1983:

1. This year we began our twenty-fifth year of operation.
2. Our enrollment is at present 385 students.
3. The enrollment figures for the past several years are:

1977-78	 313	1981-82	 347
1978-79	 310	1982-83	 370
1979-80	 334	1983-84	 385
1981-82	 338		

4. Two years ago, the Day School took over the operation of the Church's Mother's Day Out Program. Last year we were full, with 125 children in attendance on Mondays and Fridays. There were nearly 100 on the waiting list.
5. Our Mother's Day Out Program is full again this year. There are over 100 on the waiting list at the present time.
6. We have constantly tried to up-grade our program. Some of the changes include:
   a. Last year we added an Early Room. This allows parents to let students arrive at school at 7:30 a.m.
   b. Three years ago, we began an After School Program. It allows students to stay after school until 5:30 p.m. under the supervision of two adults.
   c. Three years ago, we added Art as a part of our curriculum. This year we are blessed with a new Art Room in the Activities Building addition.
   d. This year, we have hired a Mathematics Resource Teacher. This teacher will work with the teachers and students of the grade school as well as visit various elementary schools in our area.
   e. Four new computers are being purchased for use in the fifth and sixth grades. These will be used to supplement the total Day School Program and will give the students an opportunity for hands-on computer experience. As time goes on, we will evaluate the use of the computer for other grades.
   f. A revised curriculum for our four and five year old kindergarten programs is being implemented this year.
   g. A beautiful playground was built by our parents in the summer of 1982. The value of the playground is over $40,000. The cost of the materials used was $8,500.
   h. Students this year will have the use of an eating area in the new Activities Building Addition. This area will be used not only for lunches, but also for the Early Room and the After School Room Programs.
7. During the past five years, our students have taken the Iowa

Test of Basic Skills Achievement Test. During this time, our class averages as compared with other classes who took the test throughout the nation have been extremely high. In over 90% of the cases, our classes were in the 90th percentile or higher. In over 80% of the cases, our classes were in the 95th percentile or higher.

8. The good behavior of our students when they are off campus is often recognized and commented upon by persons not associated with Christ Methodist Day School.

Sam Drash stated in closing this report, "As you can see, there are many things of which we can be proud at Christ Methodist Day School. I know this is going to be a great year."

After ten years of directing Christ Methodist Day School in continued success, he submitted his resignation to accept a new position as Headmaster of the Bayside Academy, at Daphne, Alabama. We regretted losing him and his family, but we wished them every happiness in the years ahead.

In concluding the story of the Christ Methodist Day School, we quote from Sam Drash's words at the time of the Twenty-fifth Anniversary Celebration:

> For a school of the quality of Christ United Methodist Day School to have prospered for twenty-five years, there must be some major reasons. Of course the blessings and presence of God's spirit are most important. Also, the dedication and prayers of many persons have been instrumental in the school's success. Included in this group are: those on the Administrative Board who during the early years of the school helped to give it guidance; three wonderful senior ministers and their staffs who have given prayerful support and counsel to the school; the faculty, staff and administration who have worked on a day-to-day basis with the school's program through the years; the Day School's Parents Club, which during its ten years of operation, has provided many hours of service and a great deal of financial support; the Day School's Board whose members have given unselfishly of their time to see that the school runs smoothly; and the parents and their fine children whose trust in the school has been demonstrated by their physical and moral support. It is important to note that the school's program, philosophy, atmosphere and traditions have been set through many years of experience and hard work. Even though the school looks back with pride over its past, we also look forward to many more exciting years of continued growth. We know that with God's help, the school will continue to influence the lives of

many people for years to come.

Parents and Friends of the Christ Methodist Day School received a letter on June 26, 1984, from Chairman of the Board, William H. Watkins, announcing the appointment of David W. Fox as the new Director of Christ Methodist Day School. He assumed his duties as Director, July 15, 1984. David Fox has had many years of experience with elementary and pre-school children ranging from teaching in the classroom to serving as Headmaster. He began his career as a teacher in the public school system of New Orleans, Louisiana. In September 1973, he joined Presbyterian Day School as teacher and athletic director. In January 1975, he became the Assistant Headmaster and remained in that position until June 1982. For the past two years, he has been the Headmaster of Whitehaven Presbyterian Day School in Memphis. He graduated from Memphis State University in 1965 with a Bachelor of Arts degree, and a major in Health and Physical Education. Later in 1978, he received from Memphis State University a Masters degree in Elementary Administration and Supervision and a Master of Arts degree in Religion from the Memphis Theological Seminary; he has to his credit other graduate work in religion at Columbia Theological Seminary in Atlanta, as well as post-graduate study at Memphis State University. David Fox was born in Calhoun City, Mississippi, and is married to the former Mary Joan Noah. They have two sons and a daughter, Matt, Meredith and Lynn. He has been involved with athletics most of his life, coaching soccer, basketball, football, baseball and track. He has worked with Young Life for many years and has served on the Memphis City Council Young Life Committee.

The present enrollment of Christ Methodist Day School is 410 with a faculty of thirty-five persons. Approximately twenty classes are in session each day.

In addition to a number of regular events, there are two special events which the Day School looks forward to preparing and presenting: the Christmas Musical, and the Spring Musical.

Already, David Fox and his family have made a place for themselves and he is giving outstanding leadership to Christ Methodist Day School.

Note: Much of the information for this chapter of the *History of Christ United Methodist Church* is taken from the booklet prepared for the celebration of the Twenty-fifth Anniversary for the Christ Methodist Day School.

Conclusion

Wherefore by their fruits ye shall know them.
—Matthew 7:20 (KJV)

I can do all things through Christ which strengtheneth me.
—Philippians 4:13 (KJV)

As we conclude this "Labor of Love," it has been suggested that we ask three of our staff members, Dr. Charles W. Grant, Rev. Howard W. Rash, and Dr. Wayne A. Lamb, along with James H. Seabrook, Sr., who was the Chairman of the Steering Committee, to tell us where they think Christ United Methodist Church is today and also to express any projection they might have for the future.

Dr. Charles W. Grant was the first minister of Christ Church, appointed by Bishop William T. Watkins in June 1955, before there was a church. With this appointment went the challenging task of organizing and building a new Methodist Church in East Memphis in the vicinity of White Station and what is now the Laurelwood Shopping Center. He had come to the Memphis Conference in 1952 from the Crescent Hill Methodist Church in Louisville, Kentucky, and had also served with distinction the Crestwood Methodist Church, the Fort Thomas Methodist Church and The Methodist Church in Frankfort; all of these churches were in Kentucky. His other pastorates in the Memphis Conference have been Madison Heights Methodist Church and Grace United Methodist Church. Dr. Grant has always given strong emphasis to Evangelism, to Missions with an extensive outreach program and to Stewardship with an emphasis on tithing. Early in 1984, he was made

Minister Emeritus of Christ United Methodist Church. Dr. Grant's response to the question of where the Church is today and any projection for the future is succinctly stated:

> There is great satisfaction in witnessing the progress of Christ United Methodist Church — not just the increase in membership, but the extended and widened outreach, reaching into every area of life at home and far away. The deepening of the spiritual life of the congregation due to a great interest in, and participation in, prayer and honoring the Holy Spirit assures us of continued solid growth.

Reverend Howard W. Rash has the distinction of having served on the staff of Christ United Methodist Church for the longest period of time. He is now in his twenty-third year, having joined the staff as the Associate Minister to Dr. Grant in 1963. Reverend Rash came to the Memphis Conference from Simpson Memorial Methodist Church in Longbranch, New Jersey. He was the first minister from the former Methodist Episcopal Church to transfer to the Memphis Conference after unification of the three branches of Methodism in 1939. His first appointment was to St. John's Methodist Church, Memphis, as the Associate Minister. In 1943, he became the pastor of Collierville Methodist Church and served there for five years. Since his retirement he has remained on the staff of Christ Church with an assignment of Pastoral Care. He visits the members who are patients in the hospitals of the city and also makes regular calls on the shut-ins of the Church. His response to where the Church is today and his projection for the future is:

> Wonderful! sprang from my lips.
> Wonderful from the time a new Methodist Church for East Memphis was the dream of a few Methodist laymen of mid-city congregations.
> Wonderful from the time the first meeting was held in the Plaza Theater and the organization of this new group of 600 Christians took as their name, Christ Methodist Church.
> Wonderful was the rapid growth of the Church with its emphasis on Evangelism, Stewardship, Missions, and Education, who in 140 weeks moved out of the Plaza Theater and held their first service of worship in the newly constructed Fellowship Hall.
> Wonderfully glorious was the Sunday, November 1, 1964, when the congregation assembled for the first time in the newly completed Sanctuary. 'A thing of beauty and a joy forever.' What a thrill it has been and will continue to be to those who pass through

its cross-bearing doors and enter into the Joy of worshipping our Lord!

The congregation has continued to grow under the leadership of our three Senior Ministers, their staffs and the lay-coworkers. Growth, outreach ministry around the world, exciting worship services—all these are tremendous! But best of all, God is with us—lives are changed, souls are saved. Truly, it is wonderful! To God Be The Glory!

Dr. Wayne A. Lamb joined the staff of Christ United Methodist Church early in 1976, shortly after his retirement at the 1975 Annual Conference. He was engaged by the Church as Minister of Evangelism with the responsibility of Personal Visitation Evangelism. Dr. Lamb has had a distinguished ministry as he served churches in many areas of the Memphis Conference. He was the Minister of Union Avenue Methodist Church in the 1950's when they had a membership of over 2000 and when they participated as one of the sponsoring Churches for Christ Church. At the time of his retirement, he was completing his term as District Superintendent of the Memphis-Asbury District. During the ten years he has been with Christ Church, Dr. Lamb has made a significant contribution to the growth in membership of the Church. During this period the Church has received approximately 2500 members with a net gain of almost a 1000, bringing the total membership to 3800. Of this number, approximately 650, joined Christ Church on "profession of faith." Quoted is Dr. Lamb's statement in response to the questions asked:

Christ United Methodist Church with its remarkable growth, extensive outreach, and high level of spirituality is an excellent example of what God can do, does do, and will do in the life of a church when that church has competent and dedicated leadership.

From the very beginning, Christ Church has placed wholesome emphasis on Scriptural Teaching, Spiritual Devotion, Live Evangelism, World-wide Missions, Quality Education, Living Prayer and dedicated Stewardship. Christ Church has never embraced extreme liberalism or extreme conservatism, but has preached and taught vital Christianity available to everyone.

Under the magnificent leadership of Dr. Maxie Dunnam, the future of the Church grows brighter. Evidence of the moving of the Holy Spirit is seen in the expanding outreach, in evangelism, in stewardship, in fellowship, and in activities. Truly the Church is abounding in the Love of God and in service to others.

James H. Seabrook, Sr., is a successful businessman, owner of Seabrook

Wallcoverings, Incorporated. He is one of the finest of our dedicated laymen and has given many hours of his time, talents and material possessions to Christ and the Church. If anyone rereads his message in the Introduction, anyone can sense his complete dedication to his finding and following the perfect will of God for his life. He has made an oustanding contribution in writing a "Summary History" of the events in the founding of Christ Church and has traced for us and for posterity the wonderful leadings of the Holy Spirit. In response to the questions, we quote from the last paragraphs of his "Summary History":

> There are many who join a church and who unfortunately take it for granted—little do they realize that it was built on faith with the sweat, tears, and sacrifices of many others who went before them. So Christ Church stands today, having completed thirty years of history with 3800 members—$8,000,000 to $10,000,000 in buildings, grounds and equipment—virtually debt free—truly a 'venture in faith'—'an act of God'—'a miracle.'
>
> We are here today by the 'grace of God'—a five talent church returning the ten talents a beneficent Father so richly deserves—a one hundred percent return on His investment in us.
>
> Such is our heritage as we enter the second thirty-year cycle of our history.

This brings us to the completion of *The History of Christ United Methodist Church*, which we have entitled, *Christ Church, A Venture In Faith*—a title that is based on the story as told to us by James H. Seabrook, Sr.

Appendices

Appendix I
Steering Committee, 1954-1955

* Les G. Bone .... Union Avenue Methodist Church

L. Palmer Brown, III .... St. John's Methodist Church

Howard L. Davenport .... First Methodist Church

* H. W. Durham .... Trinity Methodist Church

Wm. E. Drenner .... First Methodist Church

E. C. Handorf .... First Methodist Church

* A. C. Jones .... Union Avenue Methodist Church

* C. B. Johnston............... Trinity Methodist Church

Lee B. McCormick .... St. Luke's Methodist Church

* C. R. McDaniel.............. Madison Heights Methodist Church

Samuel H. Mays .... St. John's Methodist Church

* Gerald T. Owens............. Madison Heights Methodist Church

* John A. Parsons .... St. John's Methodist Church

* Clifford D. Pierce .... Union Avenue Methodist Church

Fred M. Ridolphi .... Trinity Methodist Church

James H. Seabrook, Sr. .... Madison Heights Methodist Church

* Dr. W. J. Templeton .... St. Luke's Methodist Church

* Ed H. Tenent .... St. Luke's Methodist Church

* Deceased

Appendix II
Ministers of Christ United Methodist Church

Senior Ministers	Dr. Charles W. Grant	1955-1969
	* Dr. J. Harold Beaty	1969-1981
	Dr. Maxie D. Dunnam	1982-
Associate Ministers	Rev. B. L. Gaddie	1956-1957
	Rev. Marshall Morris	1958-1963
	Rev. Howard Rash	1963-
	* Rev. Charles H. Lynn	1967-1969
	Dr. Paul W. Clayton	1969-1974
	Rev. Edward W. Walton	1970-1976
	Rev. Albert M. Evans	1974-1977
	Dr. Wayne A. Lamb	1976-
	Rev. Robert H. Wood	1976-1979
	Rev. Catherine Wood	1976-1979
	Rev. Jerry F. Corlew	1978-1983
	Rev. Pamela McDaniel	1979-1980
	Rev. Earl A. Johnston	1983-
	Rev. James L. Loftin	1983-
	Rev. W. Edward Horton	1984-1985
	Rev. Fred C. Morton	1986-
Minister Emeritus	Dr. Charles W. Grant	1984-
Diaconal Ministers	Mr. Marvin H. Budd	1981-
	Mrs. Shirley G. Lynn	1972-
	Miss Mary Louise Caldwell	
	Mr. Clarence O. Hampton	
	Mr. Donald L. Sanford	1970-1982

* Deceased

Appendix III
Chairmen of Administrative Board of Christ Church

James H. Seabrook, Sr. 1955-1957
Howard Davenport 1957-1959
* John Parsons 1959-1961
* Edgar Tenent 1961-1963
Keith Weisinger 1963-1965
* Jesse A. Anderson, Sr. 1965-1967
Edward R. Richmond, Sr. 1967-1969
Lee B. McCormick 1969-1971
D. A. Noel 1971-1973
H. Clay Shelton, Jr. 1974-1975
John C. Whitsitt 1976-1977
Bert Ferguson 1978-1979
Gene C. Williams 1980-1981
Dr. Howard McClain 1982-1983
Jack Morris 1984-1985
Tom Dyer 1986-

* Deceased

Appendix IV
Original Trustees, Christ Church

* James Canfield   * John Parsons
Howard L. Davenport   * Dr. W. J. Templeton
* C. R. McDaniel   * Edgar Tenent

* Deceased

Appendix V
Lay Leaders, Christ Church

1955	Howard L. Davenport
1957	Dr. Howard Boone
1959	* Dr. W. J. Templeton
1961	Robert Lee Thomas
1962	Ernest Felts
1964	Bert Ferguson
1966	Dr. Tom Shipmon
1968	* Jesse Vineyard
1971	Emmett Marston
1974	Paul McQuiston
1976	Dan Farrar
1978	Orin Johnson
1980	Dr. Howard McClain
1982	Tom Dyer
1984	Dr. Richard T. Ross
1986	Jack Morris

* Deceased

Appendix VI
Membership of the First Official Board
1955-1956

James H. Seabrook, Sr., Chairman
Lee B. McCormick, 1st Vice Chairman
Fred M. Ridolphi, 2nd Vice Chairman
Charles Tate, Secretary
John A. Parsons, Treasurer
Howard L. Davenport, Church Lay Leader
Jesse Anderson
Charles Baker
Roy Barron
Earle Billings
Dr. Howard Boone
Jack Byrne
Tom Campbell
James Canfield
Hugh Carey
Jack Caskey
James Clay, Jr.
Clarence Colby
L. A. Conolly
Charles Cunningham
Howard L. Davenport
Harry DeZonia
James Doyle
Horton DuBard
Herbert Dunkman
Ray Drenner
William Drenner
Dennis Earles
J. B. Emerson
Ned French
Haskell Gass
Fred Graham
William Grumbles
E. C. Handorf
B. F. Hardin
C. P. Harris
Henry Harry
Horace Harwell
Leland Helms

John Huckabee
J. C. Ingram, Jr.
Harry Johnson, Jr.
Charles Johnston
Jesse Joyner
Keith Kelley
Frank Liddell
Porter McClean
Ralph McCool
Lee McCormick
C. R. McDaniel
W. K. Martak
Sam Mays
J. M. Meadows
Early Mitchell
York Mitchell
Earl Montgomery
D. A. Noel
R. H. Norris
Gerald Owens
John Parsons
Frank Pritchard
Sam Reid
E. R. Richmond
Fred Ridolphi
Lloyd Sarber
James H. Seabrook, Sr.
Clay Shelton, Jr.
Carey Stanley, Sr.
H. C. Stroupe
Charles Tate
Dr. W. J. Templeton
Edgar Tenent
Jesse Vineyard
Russell Weaver
Percy Whitenton
W. A. Wren
Paul Yarbrough
Mrs. Percy Whitenton

Appendix VII
Members Of Christ Church In Christian Service

Reverend Myra Bennett Antwine, Associate Minister of Raleigh United Methodist Church, Raleigh, Tennessee

Reverend William W. Barnard, Jr., Chaplain, Lourdes Hospital, Paducah, Kentucky

Florence Jo Smith Corban, Christian Education Consultant, Tupelo, Mississippi

Reverend Phillip Gates, Pastor of United Methodist Church, Batesville, Virginia

Reverend Bruce Harrington, Covenant Presbyterian Seminary, St. Louis, Missouri

Julia Atkinson Jemison, wife of Presbyterian Minister, Winter Haven, Florida

Reverend William Edward Horton, Counseling Ministry, Memphis, Tennessee

Shirley G. Lynn, Diaconal Minister, Christ United Methodist Church, Memphis, Tennessee

Fred Mills, Coordinator of Volunteer Ministries, Christ United Methodist Church, Memphis, Tennessee

Patricia Curry Simmons, wife of Baptist Minister, Memphis, Tennessee

Reverend Canon William Loyd Smith, Jr., Episcopal Cathedral of St. John, New Mexico

Judy Grumbles Sorrells, wife of Presbyterian Minister, Ellendale, Tennessee

Reverend Gerald Stigall, Minister of Christian Church, Rockwood, Tennessee

Donna Thomas, Director of Recreational Ministries, Christ United Methodist Church, Memphis, Tennessee

Reverend Ronald Thomas, Student, Emory University, Atlanta, Georgia

Nash Vickers, In Foreign Missionary Service, Zaire, Africa

Tom Marino, Assistant Youth Minister, Christ United Methodist Church, Memphis, Tennessee

Appendix VIII
President and Chairmen of the Women's Organization of Christ United Methodist Church:

Presidents of Women's Society of Christian Service	Presidents of United Methodist Women
* Mrs. Percy Whitenton 1955-56	Mrs. Jesse Anderson 1973
Mrs. Fred Ridolphi 1956-57	Mrs. H. Leroy Pope 1974
Mrs. Clarence Colby 1957-58	Mrs. Richard Ross 1975
Mrs. Ernest Felts 1958-60	Mrs. John Parsons 1976
Mrs. George Atkinson 1960-61	Mrs. Charles Johnston 1977
Mrs. Samuel H. Mays 1961-62	Mrs. Robert Utterback 1978
Mrs. John H. Tole 1962-63	Mrs. Hugh Hollon 1979
* Mrs. Edward Richmond . . 1963-65	Mrs. Curt Meierhoefer 1980
Mrs. Oscar Crofford 1965-67	Mrs. John C. Whitsitt 1981
Mrs. Orin Johnson 1967-68	Mrs. Erie S. Henrich 1982
Mrs. Keith Weisinger 1968-69	Mrs. Warren L. Simpson 1983
Mrs. Clarence Colby 1969-70	Mrs. H. Clay Shelton 1984
Mrs. S. W. Grise 1971-72	Mrs. Dwight W. Clark 1985

Chairmen of the Margaret Colby Wesleyan Service Guild

Mrs. J. Porter McClean . . . 1955-56
Mrs. Haskell Gass 1956-57
Mrs. V. A. Alexander 1957-58
Mrs. Sanford L. Jones 1958-59
* Miss Zetta Walker 1959-61
Mrs. Earl Billings 1961-63
Mrs. Avis D. Allen 1963-65
Mrs. Howard Estes 1965-67
Mrs. Francis Young 1967-68
Mrs. W. Loyd Smith 1968-70
Mrs. Thomas F. Jones 1970-72

Conference Officers From Christ United Methodist Church:

* Mrs. C. H. Henderson, also served in the Southeastern Jurisdiction and eight years on the Board of Missions.
Mrs. Oscar B. Crofford
Mrs. C. L. Woodard

Mrs. L. E. Smith
Mrs. Wayne A. Lamb, also served in the Jurisdiction and was the First Conference President of United Methodist Women.

Also listed are those who have served in various capacities of leadership
in the District:

Mrs. J. H. Tole
Mrs. Frank Pritchard
   (Mrs. C. R. McDaniel)
Mrs. H. F. DeZonia
Mrs. Ernest Felts
Mrs. John Jennings
Mrs. Dwight Koenig
* Miss Lillian Brady

Mrs. Dan Farrar
Mrs. Thomas F. Jones
Rev. Catherine Wood
Mrs. W. C. Smith
Mrs. L. E. Smith
Mrs. Robert Utterback
Mrs. Robert Condra

* Deceased

Appendix IX
Lay Delegates To Annual Conferences
From Christ Methodist Church
1956-1970

During the first fifteen years of Christ Methodist Church, the following persons served as delegates and alternate delegates to the Memphis Annual Conference; usually the first one, two or three names listed in one year were the delegates, and the others listed served as alternates:

1956
Dr. W. J. Templeton
Fred Ridolphi

1957
Dr. W. J. Templeton
W. K. Martak

1958
Dr. W. J. Templeton
W. K. Martak

1959
Dr. W. J. Templeton
Dr. Howard Boone

1960
George Atkinson
Ed Thorne

1961
Bert Ferguson
Jesse Vineyard

1962
J. H. Seabrook, Sr.
H. L. Davenport
Dr. Wm. Lovejoy

1963
Dr. Shed Caffey
Wm. H. D. Fones
Jack Renshaw

1964
J. H. Seabrook, Sr.
James Briggs
John Parsons
John Whitsitt

1965
John Tole
Charles R. Tate
Paul McQuiston
Clay Shelton

1966
Jesse Anderson
Bert Ferguson
Dwight Koenig
Lee McCormick

1967
Jack Renshaw
D. A. Noel
H. C. Ramsey, Jr.
George T. Roberts

1968
Sam Mays
Earle Billings
Ben Carpenter
Burns Landess
Henry Hottum
Harold Benson

1969
William Cazy Smith
Morris Liming
Henry Foster
Orin Johnson
C. W. Hoover, Jr.
Dan Farrar

1970
C. W. Hoover, Jr.
Dan Farrar
Orin Johnson
Dr. Winfield Dunn
Charles Tate
Emmett Marston

Appendix X
Annual Net Membership and Financial Report

Year	Membership	Budget
1956	876	$ 193,422
1957	1,119	165,635
1958	1,316	555,505
1959	1,413	235,181
1960	1,489	414,613
1961	1,579	358,848
1962	1,684	358,806
1963	1,893	463,027
1964	1,941	408,082
1965	2,091	421,410
1966	2,275	366,701
1967	2,501	400,265
1968	2,615	441,800
1969	2,592	554,144
1970	2,610	450,335
1971	2,677	209,708
1972	2,728	403,988
1973	2,745	459,376
1974	2,800	689,270
1975	2,871	524,747
1976	2,916	556,956
1977	3,067	684,375
1978	3,165	753,148
1979	3,260	864,648
1980	3,316	944,935
1981	3,396	916,365
1982	3,495	1,066,172
1983	3,571	1,100,468
1984	3,703	1,809,968
1985	3,754	1,652,566

Note: These statistics were taken from the Report made to the Annual Conference each year.

Appendix XI
Charter Members

Adams, B. C.
Adams, Mrs. B. C.
Akers, Mrs. Lawrence S.
Akin, V. Hugo
Akin, Mrs. V. Hugo
Akin, Lynwood
Alexander, V. A.
Alexander, Mrs. V. A.
Alexander, Jim
Alston, Dr. James L., Jr.
Alston, Mrs. James L., Jr.
Anderson, Jesse
Anderson, Mrs. Jesse
Anderson, Peggy (Carr)
Arnette, James B.
Arnette, Mrs. James B.

Baker, Charles W.
Baker, Mrs. Charles W.
Baker, Linda (Merritt)
Baker, Herman M.
Baker, Mrs. Herman M.
Baker, John H.
Baker, Mrs. Malcolm
Barnard, L. G.
Barnard, Mrs. L. G.
Barron, Roy W.
Barron, Mrs. Roy W.
Barron, Sandra (Stanton)
Barwick, E. C.
Bass, Mrs. Norman
Beasley, A. K., Jr.
Beeson, Billy
Bell, Warren K.
Bell, Mrs. Warren K.
Belloms, A. A.
Belloms, Mrs. A. A.
Bigger, Dr. J. F.
Bigger, Mrs. J. F.

Billings, Earle
Billings, Mrs. Earle
Birmingham, C. A.
Birmingham, Mrs. C. A.
Blackwell, Mrs. Anne G.
Blaylock, L. M.
Blaylock, Mrs. L. M.
Blaylock, David
Bland, Charles B., Sr.
Bland, Mrs. Charles B., Sr.
Bland, Charles B., Jr.
Bland, Robert C.
Bolin, A. Bryan
Bolin, Mrs. A. Bryan
Boensch, Paul
Boensch, Mrs. Paul
Bone, L. G.
Bone, Mrs. L. G. (Yetive)
Boone, Dr. Howard
Boone, Mrs. Howard
Boone, Howard A., Jr.
Bracken, William F.
Bracken, Mrs. William F.
Bramlett, Russ
Bramlett, Mrs. Russ
Brooks, Ed M.
Brown, Mrs. John
Butler, William O.
Butler, Mrs. William O.
Byrne, Jack P.
Byrne, Mrs. Jack P.
Byrne, Paul

Campbell, Dr. Charles
Campbell, Mrs. Charles
Campbell, Tom
Canfield, James T.
Canfield, Mrs. James T.
Canfield, Kenneth

Cannon, W. Carl
Cantrell, Guy
Cantrell, Mrs. Guy (Lawson)
Cantrell, William Allen
Cantrell, Barbara (Schaffler)
Carey, Hugh
Carey, Mrs. Hugh
Carloss, Leslie, Sr.
Carloss, Mrs. Leslie, Sr.
Carpenter, Ben
Carpenter, Mrs. Ben
Carpenter, Ed L.
Carpenter, Mrs. Ed L.
Carpenter, F. E.
Carpenter, Mrs. F. E.
Carter, Mrs. G. W.
Caruthers, Mrs. Roger
Caskey, Jack
Caskey, Mrs. Jack
Caskey, Jack, Jr.
Clay, Armistead
Clay, Mrs. Armistead
Clay, James N., Jr.
Clay, Mrs. James N., Jr.
Clay, James N. III
Cochran, Hunter
Cochran, Mrs. Hunter
Cockrell, Ellis
Cockrell, Mrs. Ellis
Cockrell, Creighton Allen
Colby, Clarence
Colby, Mrs. Clarence
Colby, Clarence, Jr.
Colby, Irene (Masterson)
Colvin, Frank P., Jr.
Conolly, L. A.
Conolly, Mrs. L. A.
Condra, Robert S.
Condra, Mrs. Robert S.
Copeland, Guy
Copeland, Mrs. Guy
Copeland, Nelson

Cowles, A. L.
Crawford, Mrs. J. N.
Creath, Charles J.
Crofford, Mrs. Oscar, Sr.
Crofford, Dr. Oscar, Jr.
Crosier, Mrs. J. W.
Crowley, Herschel
Crowley, Mrs. Herschel
Cullen, Hugh
Cullen, Mrs. Hugh
Cunningham, Charles
Cunningham, Mrs. Charles
Cunningham, Moody
Cunningham, Mrs. Moody
Curry, Miss Christine
Curry, James D.
Curry, Mrs. James D.

Darms, George
Darms, Mrs. George
Davenport, Howard L.
Davenport, Mrs. Howard L.
Davenport, James
Davenport, Mrs. James
Davie, Mrs. S. W.
Davis, Olen H.
Davis, Mrs. Olen H.
DeZonia, H. F.
DeZonia, Mrs. H. F.
DeZonia, Robert
DeZonia, Barry
DeZonia, Mrs. Barry
Dixon, Mrs. Floyd
Dixon, Joanne (McDowell)
Dowling, Forrest
Dowling, Mrs. Forrest
Doyle, James M.
Doyle, Mrs. James M.
Doyle, Jimmy
Drake, Robert J.
Drake, Mrs. Robert
Drake, Jennifer

Drenner, Ray
Drenner, Mrs. Ray
Drenner, William E.
Drenner, Mrs. William E.
DuBard, Dr. H. G.
DuBard, Mrs. H. G.
Duncan, James F.
Duncan, Mrs. James F.
Dunkman, Herbert
Dunkman, Mrs. Herbert
Dunn, Nat P.
Dunn, Mrs. Nat P.
Dunn, Natalie (Latham)
Dunn, Jerry
Dunn, Dr. Winfield
Dunn, Mrs. Winfield

Earles, Dennis
Earles, Mrs. Dennis
Edwards, E. O.
Edwards, Mrs. E. O.
Edwards, Elaine (Koenig)
Emerson, J. B.
Emerson, Mrs. J. B.
Emerson, Gary
Emerson, Patricia (Thompson)
Estes, Howard
Estes, Mrs. Howard

Fain, Bascom N.
Fain, Mrs. Bascom N.
Felts, Ernest
Felts, Mrs. Ernest
Ferrell, Robert S.
Ferrell, Mrs. Robert S.
Finley, Mrs. E. C. (Walker)
Fisher, Frank
Fisher, Mrs. Frank
Fisher, Ann (Mrs. Linwood Johnson)
Fisher, Robert
Flinn, Robert Reed, Jr.
Flinn, Mrs. Robert Reed, Jr.

Folsom, Mrs. H. G.
Fones, Justice W. H. D.
Fones, Mrs. W. H. D.
Ford, Mrs. K. D.
Ford, Robert
Ford, Mrs. Robert
Francis, James M.
Francis, Mrs. James M.
Fransioli, Mrs. Steve, Jr.
Fransioli, Steve III
Fransioli, Jane (Browndyke)
Frazier, John R.
Frazier, Mrs. John R.
French, Ned M.
French, Mrs. Ned M.
French, Taylor "Nick"
Fulmer, Albert, Jr.
Fulmer, Mrs. Albert, Jr.

Garber, Susan (Ozier)
Garner, Ned R.
Garner, Mrs. Ned R.
Garner, Judith (Carroll)
Garrison, Martha
Gass, Haskell
Gass, Mrs. Haskell
Gates, Jac
Gates, Mrs. Jac
Gates, Martha (Brown)
Gibson, O. F.
Gibson, Mrs. O. F.
Gibson, Jeffry
Gilbert, J. C., Jr.
Ginn, Dr. B. H.
Ginn, Mrs. B. H.
Goins, James H.
Goins, Mrs. James H.
Goldberg, Mrs. Harry
Goza, Jennings
Goyer, Dr. T. E.
Goyer, Mrs. T. E.
Graham, Fred M.

Graham, Mrs. Fred M.
Graham, Jane (Hubbell)
Graham, Mac (Fred, Jr.)
Graham, Mrs. M. O.
Graham, J. E.
Graham, Mrs. J. E.
Grant, Mrs. Charles W.
Grant, David
Grumbles, William H.
Grumbles, Mrs. William H. (Hollon)

Hall, Ernest W.
Hall, Mrs. Ernest W.
Hamer, James E.
Hamer, Mrs. James E.
Hammond, T. Jeff
Hammond, Mrs. T. Jeff
Handorf, E. C.
Holt, Mrs. George D., Jr.
Holt, Dr. Robert T.
Holt, Mrs. Robert T.
Hornsby, Martha
Horton, Frank P.
Horton, Mrs. Frank P.
Horton, Frank Lawson
Horton, William Edward
Huckabee, J. C.
Huckabee, Mrs. J. C.
Hull, Donald T.
Hull, Mrs. Donald T.
Hull, Mrs. Lee R.
Humphrey, Emma
Hunt, Charles F.
Hunt, Mrs. Charles F.
Hunter, Mrs. Willie

Ingram, J. C., Sr.
Ingram, Mrs. J. C.
Ingram, Reeves
Ingram, Mrs. Reeves

Jackman, Martha L.

Jennings, Mrs. Mae
Jernigan, C. S.
Jernigan, Mrs. C. S.
Joest, Mrs. John W.
Johnson, Harry
Johnson, Mrs. Harry
Johnson, John C.
Johnson, Mrs. John C.
Johnson, Orin
Johnson, Mrs. Orin
Johnston, Charles
Johnston, Mrs. Charles
Jones, Dr. A. M.
Jones, Mrs. A. M.
Jones, Malcolm T.
Jones, Mrs. Malcolm T.
Joyner, Jesse M.
Joyner, Mrs. Jesse M.

Kadlec, Edward F.
Kadlec, Mrs. Edward F.
Kelley, Keith
Kelley, Mrs. Keith
Kelley, David
Kenner, Jack
Kenner, Mrs. Jack
King, James Daniel
King, Merle D.
King, Mrs. Merle D.
Kite, R. R.
Kite, Mrs. R. R.
Knight, C. P.
Kyte, Mrs. Ralph

Lambert, Troy Neal
Land, T. L.
Land, Mrs. T. L.
Lawson, Sue (Hauck)
Lawson, Mrs. William V., Jr.
Lawson, William V., Jr.
Ledbetter, J. P.
Ledbetter, Mrs. J. P.

Lenz, A. W.
Lenz, Mrs. A. W.
Liddell, Frank
Liddell, Mrs. Frank
Lightfoot, Clyde S.
Lightfoot, Mrs. Clyde S.
Lightfoot, J. C.
Lightfoot, Mrs. J. C. Belle
Lindsey, Dr. Edwin L.
Lindsey, Mrs. Edwin L.
Lindsey, Ronnie
Logan, Thomas P.
Lopicolo, Mrs. Blanche
Lowe, Harry S.
Lowe, Mrs. Harry S.
Lowe, Harriet (Mansfield)

McCallum, Mrs. Lorene
McClean, Porter
McClean, Mrs. Porter
McClean, Porter, Jr.
McClean, Mrs. Porter, Jr.
McCool, Ralph
McCool, Mrs. Ralph
McCool, Martha (Young)
McDaniel, C. R.
McDaniel, Mrs. C. R.
McCormick, Lee
McCormick, Mrs. Lee
McCormick, Lee, Jr.
McGrory, Mrs. H. J.
McKinney, Joe
McKinney, Mrs. Joe (Kelly)
McKnight, William
McKnight, Mrs. William
McIntosh, R. E.
McIntosh, Mrs. R. E.
McIntosh, Marilyn (Draughon)
McIntosh, Robert Eugene
McMillan, C. H.
McMillan, Mrs. C. H.
McPhatter, William B.

McPhatter, Mrs. William B.
McVean, Charles A.
McVean, Mrs. Charles A.
McVean, Charles D.
Mankin, Dr. John C.
Mankin, Mrs. John C.
Martak, W. K.
Martak, Mrs. W. K.
Martak, Patsy (Seabrook)
Matthews, Dr. Oliver S.
Maynard, Gerald
Maynard, Mrs. Gerald
Mays, Harvey J.
Mays, Sam H.
Mays, Mrs. Sam H.
Meadows, Marion
Meadows, Mrs. Marion
Meadows, Hal
Meadows, Gerald
Mieher, W. C.
Mieher, Mrs. W. C.
Miles, Gordon
Miles, Mrs. Gordon
Miles, Lynn
Miller, Annie Wynn
Miller, Sadie A.
Mitchell, Early
Mitchell, Mrs. Early
Mitchell, Y. O.
Mitchell, Mrs. Y. O.
Montgomery, Earl
Montgomery, Mrs. Earl
Montgomery, John
Munson, Fred, Jr.
Munson, Mrs. Fred, Jr.
Murphy, J. D.
Murphy, Mrs. J. D.
Murphy, J. D., Jr.

Nason, Evelyn Kay (Baker)
Nason, Hays Len
Nason, Mrs. W. L.

Neeley, Joe P.
Neeley, Mrs. Joe P.
Newman, Mrs. LaVilla
Noel, D. A.
Noel, Mrs. D. A.
Noel, Patricia (Kelsey)
Norris, R. H.
Norris, Mrs. R. H.
Norris, Virginia
Norris, Judith
Nowlin, George
Nowlin, Mrs. George

O'Donnell, J. H.
O'Donnell, Mrs. J. H.
O'Donnell, Lynn (Roberts)
Owens, Gerald
Owens, Mrs. Gerald
Owens, Charles

Parker, Laura Lee (Ritz)
Pattinson, Jeans
Pattinson, Mrs. Jeans
Parsons, John
Parsons, Mrs. John
Payne, George R.
Payne, Mrs. George R.
Pennebaker, William B.
Peyton, Livingston
Peyton, Mrs. Livingston
Phelan, Mrs. E. J.
Pepper, Mrs. Sabra
Pierce, Mrs. Harvey
Pickens, John M.
Pickens, Mrs. John M.
Pickens, Nancy (Higgason)
Pickering, H. F.
Pickering, Mrs. H. F.
Prichard, Dr. Frank
Prichard, Mrs. Frank
Prichard, Phil
Ragsdale, Mrs. W. E.

Reeves, Russell
Reeves, Mrs. Russell
Reid, Sam
Reid, Mrs. Sam
Ricker, John B.
Ricker, Mrs. John B.
Rhodes, Mrs. Jesse T.
Rhodes, Kelley
Rhodes, Mrs. Kelley
Richards, Mrs. H. J.
Richmond, Ed, Sr.
Richmond, Mrs. Ed
Richmond, Ed, Jr.
Ridolphi, Fred
Ridolphi, Mrs. Fred
Ridolphi, Corinne (Nichols)
Ridolphi, Fred M., Jr.
Riley, Dain S.
Riley, Mrs. Dain S.
Roberds, Mrs. E. S.
Roberds, William D.
Roberts, Dr. H. C.
Roberts, Mrs. H. C.
Robinson, Dr. James A.
Robinson, Mrs. Leonese P.
Ruffin, J. E.
Ruffin, Mrs. J. E.

Samuels, Mrs. Lillian H.
Samuels, W. C., Jr.
Sarber, Lloyd
Sarber, Mrs. Lloyd
Sarber, Frances (Shearer)
Sarber, L. John, Jr.
Scates, Wilbert
Scates, Mrs. Wilbert
Schneider, W. H.
Schneider, Mrs. W. H.
Scott, Walter
Scott, Mrs. Walter (Pearl)
Seabrook, J. H., Sr.
Seabrook, Mrs. J. H., Sr.

Seabrook, J. H., Jr.
Seabrook, Mary Ann
Seabrook, Mrs. L. H.
Shelton, H. Clay
Shelton, Mrs. H. Clay
Shroyer, Mrs. E. E.
Sippel, Mrs. A. A.
Sippel, Andrew A., Jr.
Sippel, Thomas
Smith, Earl W.
Smith, Mrs. Earl W.
Smith, T. Wade
Smith, Mrs. T. Wade
Speed, B. M.
Speed, Mrs. B. M.
Spruill, Mrs. Marvin L.
Stanley, David
Stanley, Mrs. David
Stanley, C. P.
Stanley, Mrs. C. P.
Stanley, C. P., Jr.
Stanley, Mrs. R. G.
Stephenson, W. F.
Stevener, W. E.
Stevener, Mrs. W. E.
Stevener, Beverly
Stevener, Robert
Stevener, Wilfred, Jr.
Stirewalt, Martha
Stratton, R. E.
Stratton, Mrs. R. E.
Stroupe, H.C.
Stroupe, Mrs. H. C.
Stroupe, H. Clarke
Suitor, Dr. Jesse H.
Suitor, Mrs. Jesse H.
Suitor, Roscoe "Rusty"
Sullivan, C. H.
Sullivan, Mrs. C. H.
Surles, Eugene
Surles, Mrs. Eugene (Bays)
Summers, Jake A.

Summers, Mrs. Jake A.
Summers, Sylvia (Williams)

Tate, Charles R.
Tate, Mrs. Charles R.
Tate, Eloise (Foster)
Taylor, Richard G.
Taylor, Mrs. Richard
Templeton, Dr. W. J.
Templeton, Mrs. W. J.
Tenent, Ed
Tenent, Mrs. Ed
Thomas, Agnes
Thomas, Mrs. Mattie
Thomas, Mrs. F. R.
Trainor, William T.
Trainor, Mrs. William T.

Verret, Mrs. E. J.
Vineyard, Jesse M.

Waller, Mrs. Harlin E. III
Waller, James L.
Waller, Mrs. James L.
Wash, J. W.
Wash, Mrs. J. W.
Walker, Frank
Walker, Mrs. Frank
Walker, Zetta
Weaver, Russell
Weaver, Mrs. Russell
Weisinger, Keith
Weisinger, Mrs. Keith
Watson, Jack
Watson, Mrs. Jack
Walker, William H.
Walker, Mrs. William H.
Walker, Robbie
Wallace, Jack
Wallace, Mrs. Stella
Welch, Mrs. Ben
Welch, John

Welch, Mrs. John
Wellons, T. E.
Wellons, Mrs. T. E.
West, David
West, Mrs. David
West, Ann
West, David
Westbrook, A. J.
Westbrook, Mrs. A. J.
Whitenton, Percy
Whitenton, Mrs. Percy
Whitsitt, John
Whitsitt, Mrs. John
Wilkinson, John T.
Wilkinson, Mrs. John T.
Wilson, Nelson
Wilson, Mrs. Nelson

Wilson, Mrs. Ruby
Wooten, J. D.
Wooten, Mrs. J. D.
Wren, W. Albert
Wren, Mrs. W. Albert
Wright, Harry, Jr. III
Wright, Jack
Wright, Mrs. Jack

Yancey, William A.
Yancey, Mrs. William A.
Yancey, William Sims
Yarbrough, Paul
Yarbrough, Mrs. Paul

Zellner, Fletcher
Zellner, Mrs. Fletcher

Appendix XII

Description of the Sanctuary Stained-Glass Windows
R. Morland Kraus, Designer

In the LEFT CHANCEL WINDOW, the six pointed Creator's Star is seen with six concentric circles, representing the six days of Creation, while the "off-shoot" motion from each circle symbolizes an act of creation.

Below this is a burning bush remindful of the Call of Moses, while below this is the Star of David and Branch, starting our Messianic story—Jeremiah 23:5 . . . "I will raise unto David a righteous Branch and a King shall reign . . ." and Jeremiah 33:15 . . . "I will cause a Branch of righteousness to grow up unto David."

Our Lord is also referred to in the next symbol, the Rising Sun and Wings: Malachi 4:2 . . . "But unto you that fear my name shall the Sun of righteousness arise with healing in his wings."

The circle is a symbol of Eternity, while the Cross and Flag represent a banner of righteousness and justice derived from Isaiah 11:10 . . . "There shall be a root of Jesse which shall stand for an ensign of the people; to it shall the Gentiles seek: and his rest shall be glorious."

The serpent of brass is also a Messianic symbol of Jesus Christ, who in John 3:14 recognized the incident of Moses lifting up this symbol to his people while in the wilderness as a type of His crucifixion: "And as Moses lifted up the serpent in the wilderness, even so must the Son of Man be lifted up."

The water flowing below the Star of David is derived from Zachariah 13:1 . . . "In that day there shall be a fountain opened to the house of David and to the inhabitants of Jerusalem . . ." meaning a fountain for the cleansing of sin.

The Sun, Moon and twelve stars represent Jacob, his wife and twelve sons—Numbers 24:17 ". . . there shall come a star out of Jacob," while the Ladder symbolizes Jacob the Patriarch.

The Tablets represent the Old Law and the Ten Commandments, and the seven branch candlestick is a symbol of ancient Old Testament worship of which Christianity is an extension, for Jesus said in Matthew 5:17 "Think not that I am come to destroy the law, or the prophets; I am not come to destroy, but to fulfill."

The RIGHT CHANCEL WINDOW is devoted to the New Testament. At the top are the Greek letters ICXC, NIKA, meaning Jesus Christ, Victor (over Death and Sin). The XP or Chi Rho is also a Greek monogram for Jesus Christ, and within circular form may also be seen the Greek letters Alpha and Omega. "I am Alpha and Omega, the beginning and the ending, saith the Lord . . ." Rev. 1:8.

The fish is a rebus, meaning "Jesus Christ, Son of God, Saviour" which was used extensively by the early Christians.

The sun appears again, but in different form with the IHC monogram, Greek monogram for Jesus. This coincides with the Old Testament reference from Malachi 4:2.

The victorious Lamb holding the banner and standing on the book of seven seals (Revelation) is a universal symbol for Our Lord, while below is the cross representing His crucifixion. The circle on the cross contains thorns and a glorious crown suggesting that Jesus is King of Kings. Immediately below is the Easter Lily and colors of Dawn representing the purity of Christ and His Resurrection. The descending dove symbolizes the Holy Spirit and Pentecost.

At the base of the window appears the Chalice and Host representing Communion wherein He left us a memorial and commanded us—"This do in remembrance of me." Luke 22:19.

The side windows depict Christianity on the march with the pennants or banners (similar to that of the victorious Lamb) flying. The colors were selected for light control and to suggest the rich noble spirit of our faith.

THE FOUR BALCONY WINDOWS contain symbols of the four gospel writers suggested by the winged creatures in Revelation and the vision of Ezekiel. Instead of faces the open books (Gospels) appear with the names of the Evangelists.

In the "Mark" window, the designer has tried to depict the theme of the gospel as telling of a victorious leader (Christ) with the banner of victory and the Chi Rho and Greek monogram ICXC, NIKA (Jesus Christ, Victor), relating this to the Chancel. Mark's Gospel is said to have been the first which was written.

Matthew tells of Christ's lineage from the House of David (Star of David), and in this account may be found the Lord's Prayer.

Luke's Gospel relates the story of that first Christmas when the angels sang "Glory to God in the Highest"... The Nativity Star is also shown as well as the Anchor of Hope.

St. John tells of the Divine Nature of our Lord and the Kingdom of Heaven. He presents Jesus as the Messiah of the Old Testament, hence The Crown, and the victorious Lamb again appears... John 1:29 "Behold the Lamb of God..."